# JUDE

# Jude

## My Reincarnation
## From Auschwitz

JEWELLE ST. JAMES

St. James Publishing

LIBRARY AND ARCHIVES CANADA CATALOGUING IN PUBLICATION

St. James, Jewelle, 1953–
    Jude: my reincarnation from Auschwitz / Jewelle St. James.

ISBN 10: 0-9732752-1-9
ISBN 13: 978-0-9732752-1-6

    1. St. James, Jewelle, 1953–. 2. Reincarnation—Biography. I. Title

BL520.S34A3 2006        133.901´35        C2006-903034-0

Published by
St. James Publishing
P.O. Box 990
Revelstoke, B.C., V0E 2S0
Canada

Edited by David F. Rooney
Cover photo by Joshua Bortman
Author photo by Vincent Wright
Typeset by the Vancouver Desktop Publishing Centre Ltd.
Printed and bound in Canada

For my parents
Lillyean Walle and Henry John Walle

# ACKNOWLEDGEMENTS

Thank you to:

Jill Wellington, whose support and assistance literally brought *Jude* to life. Thank you, my friend!

John Baron, who guides me. I love you John.

Gertie, for sharing your heartfelt memories.

True kindred spirits—France Allion, Fran Bach, Kristy Dillon, Shelley Germeaux, Gerry Hanzlik, Kathleen Janssen, Linda Keen, Dayle Sheridan, Sarah Stewart, and Pat Wind.

Ros Staker, for the memories.

Korinn, for Poland.

Joanne and Kristy, the jewels in my life.

Raffaele Pasceri, for all you've contributed. Thanks Ralph!

David F. Rooney, whose editing genius is evident throughout *Jude*.

To Patty Osborne, who makes it all happen.

Rabbi Yonassan Gershom, whom I've never met, for writing *Beyond the Ashes*. Your words allowed me to heal.

Permission granted from Harry W. Mazal, *OBE*, The Mazal Library, A Holocaust Resource, to reproduce text from the Nuremberg Military Tribunal, Volume V. www.mazal.org

# ONE

"BIRDS DON'T FLY OVER AUSCHWITZ," she said.

Her bold statement made complete sense to me. I flew thousands of miles to see for myself the largest mass murder site in the world. Most people, sixty years later, are still horrified to enter the former death camp. Now, I was an hour's drive away, safely settled into a charming bed and breakfast in Krakow, Poland. Yet I was feeling anything but safe. In fact, as I climbed the wide stone steps to the second floor of the historic apartment building that housed the B & B, I visualized German soldiers shouting and running, emptying the building of its tenants.

After years of fear and wondering, I had finally got myself this far. My younger sister Korinn was along for support. But the next day I knew I had to face Auschwitz alone.

So, here I was, asking the owner of the B&B about the Nazi death camp.

"You may find yourself re-born after Auschwitz, yes?" she asked. She had no idea how right she would be. At the age of fifty-two, I was compelled to come. It was time to face the visions that haunted me for years.

Korinn and I had left Vancouver and flown to London

for three days of whirlwind sightseeing and shopping. She had shared my first trip to England in 1985, when I began the long search for my 17TH Century past life. After that trip, Korinn was hooked on travel and roamed the world for twenty years while I returned to England over and over.

This jaunt to London was a reunion for us; we visited Buckingham Palace, Big Ben and the Tower of London. Even though it was splendid to re-visit London, my stomach never really settled. I knew the fun would end; I would have to face the darkness.

The London leg of our trip ended too quickly and I battled the feeling of dread as I waited at Gatwick airport for our trip to Krakow. People were scattered about the waiting room for the same flight. My eye caught an eerie sight, and my heart started to pound. I was staring at a young gentleman, a twin—practically—of a man I have seen in other places. Was he a spirit? I didn't know and that fueled my tension.

I didn't tell Korinn for I knew she would think I was losing my mind but I had seen his look-alike before, once in England, once in California. He had sandy blonde hair, blue eyes, and a slight bump on his Roman nose. He was identical to John Baron, a man I knew in a past life in 17TH Century England. I spent twenty years of my life tracking down the ways his past life intertwined with my own and I wrote my first book about our past life together. Yes, I was stunned to see him on this flight. But settling back in my seat as the plane took off I forgot about him. As I closed my eyes childhood memories washed over me.

My rural home in British Columbia in the 1950s and 60s was a kaleidoscope of earthy aromas, thickets of pine trees stabbing at the clear sky, and an endless sparkling lake where the Shuswap Indians used to hunt and fish. My grandma's second cousin was the first white man to inhabit the north side of the lake, but this piece of family history didn't impress us much as kids.

I remember the summers; my brother Norm and I yearned to water-ski all day and pestered our dad as soon as he came home from work to take out the boat before the sun went down. Many a moonlit night, my cousins and I would sleep on the beach in front of my grandma's house. The lake at midnight was smooth as glass and the only light streamed from the moon, illuminating a soft glow over the mountain tops. The drone of motor boats and the raucous happy sound of children laughing would resume in the morning but at night, the scene was age old, hankering back to the days when the natives lived here.

Another time, another sleep-over, on the beach at my friend Daphne's summer home, I awoke in the wee hours of the morning. I lay there listening to the water gently lapping the shore. I glowed with contentment. Who would think my picture-post-card childhood would soon be tarnished by the ugliness hidden deep in my sub-conscience?

I cried when we moved away from the lake. Yoho National Park in the Rocky Mountains near Lake Louise and Banff was now our new home. My grandma said we were lucky to have spectacular scenery for our entire childhood and only now do I understand her statement. We had more than fresh air to breathe, wild animals sleeping on our lawn, and aquamarine rivers . . . we had innocence, yet some how the horror of the Holocaust began to invade the tranquillity.

When I was ten I read a pocket book about it, but today I only remember one scene: 1940s Europe, the land was flat and brown. Stick-thin prisoners wearing striped clothing, trudging with shoulders hunched and shaved heads bent, were enclosed by an endless high, slightly curved barbed wire fence. Nearby townspeople, risking punishment, threw marmalade over the fence to the bony, out-stretched hands below. The prisoners cried with joy as the marmalade sky rained gold from heaven. The scene broke my heart, and my obsession was born.

Years later, I was riveted to the television when black-and-white newsreels from *World War II* showed mountains of dead, emaciated bodies bulldozed into open pits. The narrator said the dead were Jews. I felt an odd connection.

In 1967, the summer of love, I started my first job. I was so excited and enjoyed working as a waitress. My boss was gruff, yet I suspected he had a soft heart underneath. My friend at work was a sassy waitress named Sue. Just looking at her red, teased hair with a pencil tucked in the bun, made me smile. One day the boss growled at Sue to pick up her order. As Sue balanced plates of warm pancakes on her arm she muttered, "Dirty Jew." Suddenly I felt ill and was glad our boss didn't hear her. I felt ashamed, as though the words were directed at me and working in the restaurant lost its appeal.

The next summer brought a new job. Teens from all over British Columbia lodged in the alpine wood cabins surrounding the resort, and work became the social scene. The winter, although quieter than summer, provided an after-school job that was thrilling, especially when the Canadian National ski team came to stay while training in nearby Lake Louise. I remember serving Nancy Greene's future husband, Al Raine, a cup of tea and being disappointed that Nancy had the flu and I had missed meeting her.

The owners of the resort lived in Calgary and it was months before I met them. When I was finally introduced to the German proprietors, I felt a mixture of confusing emotions. The owner's wife was charming and lovely, and perhaps her husband was, too. I can only remember his German accent that sounded to me, like a barking dog. I avoided him, but I couldn't escape the new German chambermaid. Her accent stirred emotions within me ranging from fear to anger.

One day, we were cleaning a room together, and for no reason, I snapped. "Why?" I shouted. "Why did your countrymen kill all the Jews? No one helped. No one cared. Why? Why?"

She looked stunned and we both burst into tears. "We didn't know," she sputtered. "We just didn't know."

"Bull *shit!*" I screamed.

Then in 1980, John Lennon was murdered and my world tumbled down. Through an amazing odyssey of hypnosis, visions, and dreams I began a past-life search that led me back to the 1600s in England. It took me two decades to piece it all together and I eventually found ancient records to substantiate the amazing truth. I had lived a past life with the soul that became John Lennon. Through searching for that past life, I slowly began to realize my obsession with the concentration camps was perhaps also a past life.

Uncovering passionate love in ancient England was one thing but you couldn't pay me to undergo a past-life regression to Germany where I suspected I lived during the Holocaust. My John Lennon search devoured twenty years of my life. I couldn't fathom starting another search. But fate would lead me to face the fear.

The man I knew and loved in 17TH Century England, John Baron, began communicating with me around the year 2000 through automatic writing. I would wake from a sound slumber and words would flood my mind. I would leap from my bed and scrounge for paper and pen to capture the torrent of words. One night, he gave me a poem about the Nazi death camps. That's what led me to this plane trip that would soon land me in a frightening place I was afraid to face.

Korinn awoke as we began our descent into Krakow. We pressed our faces to the aircraft windows absorbing the view—slightly rolling snowy hills enshrouded with fog. The steps from the plane led to a shuttle bus waiting to take us to the terminal. The ride took minutes, but seemed longer for the John Baron look-alike was sitting beside me. When the shuttle bus arrived and we herded into the airport, I turned and he was gone. His presence boosted my courage; he was a sign that I wasn't alone.

After clearing customs a young man met us, our driver from the B&B. He conversed in broken English which was wonderful since we spoke no Polish. He was a young university student and drove for tourists whose fees paid his way through school. We were grateful for our chauffer as we never would have found our B&B in the centre of Krakow on our own. His van whipped up and down wide streets lined with huge aristocratic buildings that would have been beautiful except for graffiti and peeling paint. I could visualize German army tanks on the dark streets and nearly every building looked like Gestapo headquarters.

"You're imagining that," Korinn said.

Thank God she was with me. It took all my strength to keep my emotions in check, and I was happy to let her deal with the practical side of things like reading maps and counting Zlotys.

The next morning, after a delicious breakfast of meat, cheese, rolls and strong coffee I was ready to tackle the unthinkable. I decided to travel to Auschwitz alone. Korinn planned a happy day touring a castle, and I knew that if there was ever a time in my life to be strong this was it: November 21, 2005.

Our landlady at the B&B, after hearing of my wish to travel alone to Auschwitz suggested I hire her driver, the same young man who had picked us up at the airport.

A guest at the B&B suggested I travel by train to Auschwitz as millions of Jews had done. No, I couldn't do that. My thoughts, however, on the one hour drive to Oswiecim, the Polish name for Auschwitz, were with the millions who were forced to travel to their deaths by rail.

The sky was grey and wet snow fell as I anxiously watched the barren Polish countryside through the van window. Again I thought of the Jews who had traveled this route, crammed into locked, dirty cattle cars, traveling for days with no food or water, from ghettos across Europe. Their only view was through the wooden slats of the boxcars, and I felt guilty riding in comfort, toasty in my wool coat and gloves and scarf. The weather matched my dismal day.

When I returned to the B&B that night, I was unable to speak and felt lucky to spy a lone computer in the front lobby. My fingers clicked over the keys as my emotions poured into an email for friends back home, feelings I couldn't verbalize.

*Dear Friends,*

*I finally made the trip to Auschwitz today and felt an urgent need to write it all down for I don't want to forget any of what I experienced today. Bear with me as I unload on you.*

*I started my tour in* Auschwitz One *where political prisoners mostly, were kept. Now, the many red brick barracks are a museum. I walked under the infamous sign* Arbeit Macht Frei—*translated,* Work Shall Set You Free, *one of the numerous stupid Nazi slogans used in the Holocaust. I walked for a few meters and was feeling alright, like maybe I could do this. Then I smelled something acrid in the air. A man stood beside one of the barracks. I approached him asking if he spoke English.*

*Yes, he did.*

*"What is that awful odor in the air?"*

*"What odor?" he asked.*

*"It's hard to explain," I said, and asked if he could smell it.*

*He shook his head, and in the gentlest voice I ever heard he said, "Perhaps it's a special scent for you, yes?"*

*I nodded yes, and thanked him. I turned away so he wouldn't see my tears but he was busy wiping snow from his granny glasses. Leaving the kind man and entering a barrack I wiped away more tears. It seemed fine to quietly cry here, I wasn't the only one. The piles of hair, suitcases, and shoes taken from the murdered Jews were unreal. Photos of prisoners lined the hallways. I stared into their eyes, realizing they were real people living sixty years ago in civilized Europe.*

*I wandered through the rows of barracks and more scents assaulted my senses. They would last thirty seconds and then disappear. Once, I smelled burning hair. I turned away from the spot and it disappeared. I returned, it recurred.*

I paused in my typing. This email wasn't the time to share the Hebrew letters. The signs outside each barrack explaining its history were in three languages; Polish, English and Hebrew. I gasped when I recognized the Hebrew letters, but I would explain later.

*I lost track of time. It was all surreal. As I walked, I psychically saw, or visualized, row upon row of prisoners. The scenes were all in black and white, actually brown and white, marching beside me yet as if they were in another dimension. It was like I was with them but they didn't see me. I was awash in the creepy sensation.*

*Between two barracks were a courtyard and a wall aptly named* The Killing Wall. *Thousands of prisoners were shot here. I stood alone at the wall, now adorned with flowers and candles, and heard my voice involuntarily call, "Papa!"*

*Then, clear as any sound I ever heard, my Papa's voice arose from the past. "Remember the importance of the written word, my child; you must remember!"*

*The driver was waiting and he took me to the second camp* Auschwitz-Birkenau, *a camp created strictly for killing. I knew the trains pulled in here, and immediately upon arrival the selection process began. An orchestra would play classical music, relaxing the large crowds of unsuspecting Jews while the black-uniformed SS, did their deplorable "sorting."*

*Children under fifteen, young mothers, old people, weak and ill people were sent straight to the gas chambers. Those strong enough to work for the Nazis were allowed, for awhile anyway, to live. These "lucky" ones were sent to barracks.*

JEWELLE ST. JAMES

*I arrived at Auschwitz-Birkenau and walked about a quarter mile before arriving at the intersection where the selection process took place. I found myself walking with a large group of people, on the same road that ran parallel to the train tracks that brought Jews here sixty years ago. At first, I strolled with the group, then slowly began to notice they were wearing clothing like army fatigues. Most were men, but some were women. I noticed they wore armbands with the now familiar Hebrew letters and in English it said* Israel. *A man who walked beside me had a rolled up flag and I could make out the Star of David. They were Jews! Only when we reached the selection place did I realize the Jews and I had entered the death camp together. Exactly how I would have arrived in 1944.*

*Finally I broke away from the group and entered the barracks alone, wandering from one to the other. It was dusk, the snow was biting, and the barracks were becoming dark. I tread through them anyway. The bunk beds were in triple levels, many with a dried rose or flower left by someone. I wished I had a flower to leave, but instead kissed my fingers and gently lay my hand on a bunk.*

*I returned to the selection spot, crossed the railway tracks and entered the massive area where row upon row of brick chimneys remain. There was no one in sight. I cried and I heard myself whisper, "My God."*

*Suddenly, I had a flashback to age ten, standing by the lake and vowing that one day I would go to Europe. Today was the day.*

I paused in the typing, then added:

*Tomorrow, I return to Auschwitz with my sister. No doubt it will be a different day, in what way it's hard to guess.*

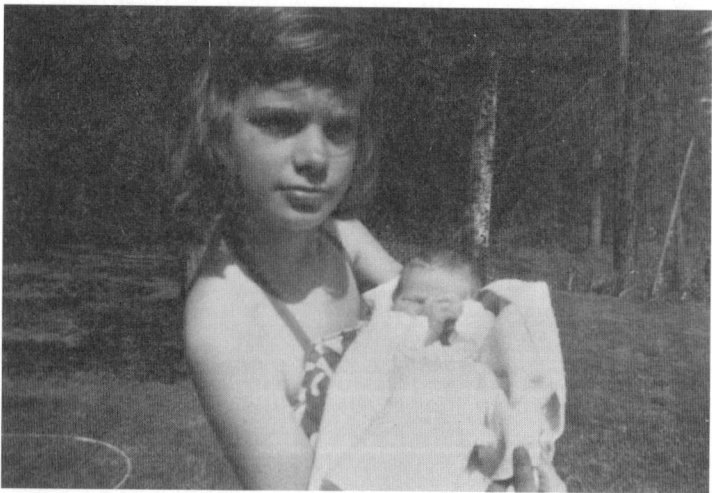

*Jewelle age 10*

# Two

EXHAUSTED FROM THE PROFOUND DAY in the death camp, I slowly rolled my neck and aching shoulders trying to ease the heaviness I felt as I clicked off the computer. My body felt weighty as I trudged up the stone steps and slipped quietly into our dark room. Korinn breathed loudly in peaceful slumber. I envied her. I quickly undressed, discarding my clothes in a heap on the floor. I could almost smell Auschwitz, its odors clung to the fabric and I shuddered. My muscles protested as I crawled into the narrow bed and twisted my body to find warmth and comfort. I'm so weary, I thought. Yet despite my physical need for sleep, I lay there staring into black space. My mind slipped back in time.

My precious sister Konni flashed into view and I smiled faintly. Konni lived in southern California, and was held prisoner in her bed with Multiple Sclerosis. Konni and I talked nearly every day by phone. She was always bright and happy and only once did I hear a catch in her voice on her thirty-eighth birthday. It had been ten years since she walked, she said. Her dream was to dance across her kitchen. For years, I lived with guilt wondering why she got the MS gene, or whatever it was, and I was healthy.

Konni was my candle, shedding light on my grief over the death of John Lennon. As illness ravaged her body, her psychic abilities blossomed. In a vision, she saw me in a tiny town called Petworth in ancient England with a man named John Baron. This information ignited my passionate search for the truth of that past life, and her continued psychic flashes assisted my efforts to discover the proof.

Strange things started to happen when we talked by phone. My call display screen began displaying symbols that appeared and flashed when I spoke with Konni. I called the phone company because the call display wouldn't work for a day after one of these bouts, but they were as puzzled as I. My friend Cindy suggested I copy down the symbols, and she later agreed, they were weird and didn't resemble any letters or numbers we'd ever seen.

While Konni tuned into my past life in the 1600s, *another* past life from the 1940s appeared to her. I had never told Konni about my concentration camp obsession as she was five years younger than me, and besides, I never discussed it with anyone. Now she was sharing fascinating snippets about a life in 1940s Germany . . . an existence I already sensed.

She described the Black Forest region of Germany and explained that my family was involved with the Resistance. Supposedly, we were part of a huge underground, secretly and dangerously transporting people out of Germany. The idea of a resistance family was only a passing thought, if there even *was* such a family.

JEWELLE ST. JAMES

I was still in a fervent search for my life with John Baron. My love was so intense that I felt addicted at some level, so paid little attention to Konni's 1940s vision.

I once heard, "While the music plays, there is music in the silence between the notes." This rang true when my German life began showing itself as I obsessed over the events from my past life in England.

Our favorite family restaurant was called the *Black Forest Inn*, an Austrian eatery with a European atmosphere. The music, the food, the ambience—even the elaborate cuckoo clock—felt oddly familiar. It was a place of comfort, too, and strangely, when my husband and I divorced, we made a promise never to share it with another mate.

On Sundays, I don't know *why* Sundays, I would place Johann Strauss on the stereo and play it all day. *The Blue Danube* especially tore at my heart. The beautiful waltz, like the *Black Forest Inn*, was *very* familiar. It was bittersweet, like love and hate, life and death.

Then there was the European deli where I just liked to *be*. I wandered the shop delighting in the yeasty, sugary aromas and pausing to examine every European product. I reveled in the sights, sounds and feelings they evoked, filling my senses. At Christmas I always bought the stollen, a German fruit bread sprinkled with white sugar. One year, the deli ran out of stollen. My heart lurched and with great effort I made it to the safety of my car before bursting into tears of frustration. I couldn't imagine Christmas without stollen.

Later, my friend Herma said, "You really should pay attention to that strange reaction."

Throughout this period in the 1980s, I belonged to a women's group. We had *secret sisters* which meant that on special occasions you bought your sister an anonymous gift. My *sister's* birthday was approaching, and I loved shopping for those secret given gifts. As I shopped, nothing seemed right. Then I saw it! The most beautiful candle holder I had ever seen. My heart filled with joy as I purchased the perfect present. That night I proudly showed my husband.

"Is she Jewish?" he asked.

I looked at him like he was crazy. "Why would you ask that?"

"You bought a menorah!"

"What's a menorah?"

"It's a religious candlestick—one of the oldest symbols of Judaism."

I'd never heard of menorah, and I didn't care if it had a name, to me it was just the most precious thing I had ever seen. Little did I know the gift was really for me.

My phone banter with Konni continued as I was physically shown examples or memories of these past lives. Once, Becky, a psychic, suggested I keep a journal and write down all conversations with my sister. I laughed. I didn't know then that Konni would die and leave me. I wish I had taken Becky's advice. My beloved sister passed away in September of 2000. I was devastated and Herma consoled me over tea in my apartment. As we silently sipped the hot brew, I casually glanced out the window at a stopped train. The heavy locomotives chugged daily close to my apartment window. Some days the clanging noise irritated me, yet in an odd way, it was familiar and comforting. This day, in my melancholy state, my eyes fell upon the side of a boxcar. I was dismayed to see *Konni* spray painted in large block letters. Only three days had passed since her passing. Was I imagining her name painted on the side of a train? Herma confirmed it, the letters on the boxcar said *Konni*.

Seven days later, I received my first message from Konni. It was the first time I had ever channeled a spirit. I sat at my kitchen table doodling with a pen on a piece of paper, and wrote, *Konni, if there's something that you'd like to say please feel free to use this pen.*

The pen suddenly felt light and airy and, within two minutes, the first word appeared.

*Tell the story, Jewelle, of your past life which is not even the past. It's all now, it's all one life. We think our lives are separate; It's all one play, one picture.*

*Tell of your past life and how it's part of you now. That's why it's part of you now because nothing ends. You take off your clothes at night, but you're still there. Later your body dies, but your soul is still there—just changing elements. Body to body, which has nothing to do with your soul which is never ending.*

*Tell your story so others can see where their lives are; what is their big picture. That is what departed souls are trying to tell people on earth. You should see all the souls trying to communicate with their loved ones. Its so simple. We're not parted any more than when a child goes to school and returns at night. We are all in different schools.*

*There is no heaven, where I am. There is no heaven, no hell, just another classroom.*

*Love,*
*Konni*

I cried for my sister. Confined in a frozen body for a decade, imprisoned in bed, she was now free. How could I feel sad at her death, when her messages were filled with such joy?

A month passed before I heard from Konni again.

*I'm starting to slip away from the planet's sphere. I've slowed down in my playing, but playing I still do. I feel so light, so clear. This earth life, Jewelle, is not to be taken too seriously. If you want to accomplish something all you have to do is create it, but lightly - nothing is meant to be difficult.*

*We own no one, and no one owns us. A hardship is created by people and possessions. All those people with bank accounts—passed over spirits shake their heads at all the money concerns. They are also shaking their heads at themselves, for no soul is judged by anyone but themselves.*

Konni then wrote personal messages to family members and ended her letter saying *John smiles, he's here too —he's cool, and as you know, I am too!* Konni had no qualms about telling family members that *she* was the cool one. I smiled to see that her personality, although in spirit, was still alive.

One night a few months later, I lay down on my bed ready to greet sleep. It was midnight, and rain pounded against my bedroom window. Instead of shutting off the lamp, I reached in my bedside table for a pen and notebook. I was suddenly in the mood for a conversation with Konni. No need for a phone, I simply talked to her in my mind while casually poising the pen over the pad of paper.

My pen began to write.

*Hello, dear sister, yes, I am fine and well. I am studying with teachers. John is here, in fact he's interrupting me and wants to use your pen.*

At that point John Baron, my 17TH Century soul mate, came through, and he called me by my ancient name Katherine. I was shaking with excitement.

*Katherine, I'd like to speak to you of Petworth.*

Sure, my thoughts replied, we can talk about Petworth. What about it?

*Petworth, our beautiful Petworth, is not all that you think it is, Katherine. I have something to tell you, I don't know if you can handle it.*

"Of course I can handle it," I said with confidence. "What can be so bad about Petworth?"

*Please forgive me Katherine—I'm not sure you are ready for facts. You do repeat; all your clues are in your current life.*

Now, I was frustrated. It was the year 2001. Certainly I could deal with any antiquated problem from the 1600s. I was disappointed John left me hanging. I wondered how long I would have to wait for him to share his bad news with me.

Suddenly, with a jerk, my pen began to write with such ferocity that my fingers struggled to keep up. The pen raced across the page for two minutes. The writing came so quickly I had no time to read the sentences until it was finished. I was astounded, the entire passage was a melodic poem. Only then did I read the truth. A horrific truth.

*World War II was time of fear*
*Where love was abandon and never was near*
*Heinrich and Greta, your parents were named*
*Katarina, my love, your name is the same*

*The barracks, the stench, the hatred, the fear*
*Hell hell hell, the burning, the screams*
*No, my darling, that was not a dream*

*German you were, a Jew as well*
*I was the soldier, you in the cell*
*You were in prison, I was your guard*
*I loved you, I shot you, to save you from hell*

*Please forgive me, I know that you do*
*My life is unfolding, here are some clues*
*Barbed wire and lights, black bread only to eat*
*We danced to the music, light on our feet*

*No one was watching, your eyes I still see*
*Laughing and loving and crazy for me*
*I had to shoot you Katie*
*I knew your fate*
*Of torture, of hunger, of rape after rape*

*I had to stop the horror to follow*
*My love for you saved you, by ending your life*
*My darling, I had to, you had once been my wife.*

I was stunned. The story was foreign, yet familiar. Bitter, yet sweet. I longed for more.

# THREE

AFTER THE POEM I could no longer deny that another past life was showing itself. I had asked for additional information, and more bloomed like seeds buried and dormant for years. My prosaic life in tiny Revelstoke, British Columbia seemed an odd garden for these seeds, especially my rather mundane job. I took a home healthcare course when I was married, and worked as a travelling nurse's aide for ten years. My chores ranged from washing dishes and house work to caring for dying patients in their homes. It wasn't long before I realized it was the same occupation I worked at three hundred years ago in Sussex, England. History does like to repeat itself.

Through my work, I met hundreds of elderly folk, and they were all great teachers. My new *clients*, as the system calls these seasoned sages, were Mikel and his wife Mila.* I first met them in their backyard on a sunny September afternoon. Their 1950s-style ranch house was surrounded by lilac bushes with a shed in the back and majestic mountains looming in all directions. It was their home for fifty years after leaving war-torn Europe.

* *Not her real name*

JEWELLE ST. JAMES

Mikel loved the sun, and a deep tan accented his sky blue eyes.

At ninety he was still a handsome man. Mila was petite, her chocolate eyes a bit distant. She loved dancing. As her Alzheimer's progressed, her inner child returned. With new-found innocence, she would now wholeheartedly waltz around the kitchen with me. Mikel affectionately called his wife *Young Lady*.

For two years I visited every Sunday afternoon to administer Mila's medication, sometimes to dance, but mostly to learn.

Their life stories emerged during the time I cared for Mila and I was fascinated by their Polish roots. After fifty years in Canada, they remained proud Poles and their conversation bounced from English to Polish. Mikel and Mila had lived through the war, and for them, *World War II* was only yesterday. It took me months to realize that "living through the war" meant Mikel spent time in a prisoner-of-war camp, and Mila was forced to leave her parent's home to work in a German factory.

As I dusted their living room, Mikel described a ghastly era in his home country and beyond as the Nazis implemented *The Final Solution*, their plan to eliminate all Jews from Europe.

Mikel's blue eyes narrowed as he shared his story. He told how *the Jews*, according to Hitler, were to blame for all hardships from Germany's defeat in *World War I* to the country's economic hardship.

"Jews at this time, in the 1930s, composed only one

percent of Germany's population, but German Jews considered themselves German by nationality and Jews only by religion," Mikel explained. "Long before the war began in 1939, laws were implemented in Germany (Nuremberg Laws of 1935) which deprived Jews of their German citizenship. Jews were removed from schools, banned from professions, and were even forbidden to share a park bench with a non-Jew."

I set down my dust rag, visibly shaken now. The story set off disturbing emotions from deep inside me. How in the Hell could modern Europe just sixty years ago during my own parent's lifetime, reduce the Jewish people, fellow German citizens, to the status of animals? I tried to imagine how my own neighbors, friends, family, and co-workers would react if we were suddenly treated like dogs by our government and our own countrymen. I was thoroughly appalled.

It would take many visits to Mikel and Mila's house for more details to spill out. I was always drawn in, yet repulsed at the same time. I learned that the bullying started slowly at first. Jews' driver's licenses were suspended. Civil service jobs eliminated pensions for Jews. The government confiscated radios, and curfews banned Jews from the street. New rules permitted Jews just one hour a day to shop for their needs. And when Jews were on the street, they were subjected to random beatings.

Mikel explained how the abuse intensified. Jews over the age of six were forced to wear a *Star of David* badge—a yellow six pointed star with the block letters

*JUDE*, the German word for Jew, for easy identification. The yellow badge made a distinction. One day they were just people on the street, and the next day they were Jews or non-Jews.

Mikel continued. "If an *SS* official decided the Star was sewn slightly crooked on their coat, they were beaten. Actually the *SS* needed no reason to beat a Jew and they encouraged fellow Germans to do the same."

The yellow star frightened me. I couldn't imagine wearing such an atrocious badge today. I shook my head in disgust. I later looked it up on the Internet and the glaring yellow star raged at me from the computer screen.

During another visit, I dutifully dispensed Mila's medicine, then immediately pulled up a chair next to Mikel. As much as I hated hearing about the atrocities, I had a compelling need to hear the truth about the Holocaust, and I knew at some level that Mikel was fertilizing one of those dormant seeds. This day, I ignored the housework. Mikel now enjoyed sharing his stories.

He resumed, "*JUDE* was scrawled on Jewish shops in Berlin to deter people doing business with *the enemy*. Then the government forced Jewish entrepreneurs to hand over their businesses to non-Jews, the so called Aryan race."

In books I read Hitler imagined the Aryan race, what he called a pure race of blonde-haired, blue-eyed super people. So what started as small stumbling blocks for the Jews, became gas chambers for millions.

In 1950, Mikel, who had left Europe after the war,

returned for Mila asking for her hand in marriage and to bring her to Canada.

"This best place in the world, this Canada," Mila would say in broken English, waving her hand.

Listening, week after week, to Mikel's war-time memories compelled me to dig the *World War II* channeled poem out of a drawer and read it again carefully. Each line was mesmerizing, but always the skeptic I needed to find proof of its meaning. I could only believe the poem really *did* tell the story of a past life if like a detective, I could discover indisputable facts.

One line was definitely foreign to me, so it was a good place to start. *Black bread only to eat.* I had never heard of black bread. Did it really exist in the concentration camps? Was that really all they ate?

I stopped at a favorite café while pondering black bread and if such a bread existed. The café, called the *Alphaus*, was run by a German family and was a casual version of the *Black Forest Inn*. I ordered the sinfully delicious home-made apple strudel and wondered how on earth I could find information about black bread. I absentmindedly watched the elderly owner, who was the restaurant's cook and baker, shuffle to the booth in front of me. I nearly burst out laughing at myself. I needed information about black bread in Europe, and a German baker was sitting three feet away.

My heart started to pound at this sudden coincidence. I asked the waitress, the owner's wife, if I could speak with him.

"Of course." she said, beckoning me to her husband's table.

I asked him if he had ever heard of black bread and he instantly started explaining how it is made. His words blurred as he described the process of grinding the grain, and explained how each region of Europe bragged their own distinct styles of bread.

"The long story short, black bread was a dark rye or pumpernickel," he said.

Would black bread be part of a concentration camp diet? The question was ready to spew from my tongue. But the baker was German, possibly the age to have painful memories. I hated to intrude, so I spared that gentle man the questions that burned in my mind.

Still, I was elated that someone had explained black bread to me. One line of the poem was now substantiated by a person who had actually baked black bread in Germany. I knew this investigation was in full throttle even as the subject seemed way beyond my level of endurance. Who wants to remember a terrifying past life? Obviously I did because I was still hungry for more clues to investigate.

I re-read each line keenly then remembered that when I first channeled John Baron, right before he dictated the poem, he had mentioned our Petworth life. I thought of my friend Ros. I had met her on my first trip to Petworth in 1990, when I was researching my past life in the 1600s. Ros helped me with local history as I proved the reality of that past life, and we became fast friends. I have returned to England often, probably as much to visit her as for past life reasons. Ros and her husband also came to Canada and I loved showing them spectacular British Columbia. They were like family.

Now she was on my mind again, so I wrote her a chatty letter, and added a P.S. saying I was investigating the concentration camps in Germany.

Strange things happen to me when I visit Petworth. On one journey to Petworth, Ros and I took a stroll around the town at dusk. The sky's pinkish glow illuminated the bursting flower boxes on the windowsills of colorful stone cottages. Suddenly I was overcome by a waft of smoke so thick I could barely breathe.

"There it is Ros," I exclaimed. "The smoke. That's the smell I've been telling you about."

"There's nothing in the air, Jewelle," she said a bit annoyed. She had heard me talk of the smoke smell before.

"But, but," I sputtered, the smoke thick in my throat.

Ros repeated firmly, "There's no smoke."

She would have to say that often because every time I was in Petworth, I smelled the smoke. As Ros' irritation grew, I eventually stopped mentioning it. Yet, an hour before the taxi was to take me to Heathrow, I ran down to the town's square for a quick goodbye. Again, I could smell smoke and I truly wondered whether it was my imagination. Then I overheard two ladies who were puzzled by the smoky odor on such a warm day. The smell of smoke was only one of many strange sensations that I'd shared with Ros over the years, and she was used to the notion that my life was one long mystery in need of resolution. As I posted the letter I wondered if my past life in a concentration camp would interest her.

# FOUR

$A$s THE SEEDS PLANTED DEEP in my subconscious mind began to sprout, the amazing coincidences leading to my past life in 1940s Germany multiplied. It was at the time I met my dear friend Jill Wellington. Jill is an author from Michigan and our paths crossed on the Internet during an author's forum. We started e-mailing every day and soon our chats grew into a rich friendship.

Jill was a television news reporter for many years and enjoyed coincidences so amazing and meaningful, she began to study the phenomenon called *synchronicity*. She and her mother wrote a mystery novel entitled *Fireworks* that showed the synchronicity in action. Jill sent me the book and I devoured it. I could finally understand the compelling synchronicities in my own life.

Jill told me the spirit world shows her the same sign over and over, a sort of proof or comfort signal. She always sees the number 111 on clocks, addresses, room numbers . . . everywhere. She sees the magic number every day and is often awakened at 1:11 in the morning.

Hearing about Jill's 111 sign, I finally understood my dimes. I have been finding dimes, or they have found me, for more than ten years. The first time I noticed them was when I walked out of my daughter's boyfriend's house on the way to my car. At least a dozen dimes were scattered across his driveway. Sort of like pennies from heaven, but these were dimes. I didn't pay much notice. Within days, I started finding them everywhere. I was still married at the time and my husband even began commenting, "Oh, there's a dime for you," as they appeared on the floor all around our house. When we separated, the dimes continued in my new home and new town. They would often show up when I needed comfort or confirmation, and my dime fairy also had a sense of humor.

When I started home care, my first assignment was looking after some children for a week while their mother was in the hospital. They lived on a farm far up the side of a mountain. Strangely, I thought no dime could find me up that high. Five minutes later, on their doorstep I found a dime. I wagged my head in amazement as I know it wasn't there earlier.

Another time, I grumbled when a client asked me to vacuum her huge house. The lady was bed-bound with Multiple Sclerosis. I glared at her husband plopped on a chair watching television. Why couldn't he help out? Just then, I spotted a newspaper on the lady's bedroom floor with a dime laying on a headline that blared, *Women Still do all the Work*. Thanks for the confirmation, dime fairy, I thought with a laugh. Do you vacuum too?

My first Christmas as a single person was a difficult time. Christmas morning I drove through heavy snow to my daughter's house and on the way I stopped at a corner store to pick up some juice. My heart was heavy as I opened the door, bracing myself for the assault of frosty air. Just as my boots landed in the fresh snow, something caught my eye. Half-buried in the powder was a dime. Where did it come from? Now my heart was warmed by the dime fairy's Christmas present, the best I received that year.

Later, I moved and worked for two years in a restaurant. The job was challenging and I was distraught. Dimes poured from every direction. Yet, with the cash register chinking every few minutes I figured loose change would scatter a bit. Finally, I asked the other workers if they found dimes. None ever did.

One year nearly one hundred dimes crossed my path.

My cousin Dayle suggested I start journaling the dates, number of dimes, and what was happening in my life when I found one. For two more years I kept a journal. The first year I found sixty-eight dimes, the second year sixty-nine dimes.

Now Jill was telling me my dimes were definitely a sign from the spirit world. I wondered if the dime fairy is my beloved John Baron who had already invaded my earthly life. I know now that John guided my research, travels and writing for my first book.

When the manuscript was ready for printing I was afraid and vulnerable. I had no idea how to publish a book, but knew it was my mission. Dimes abounded throughout the publishing journey in stores, the post office, the street. No one else seemed to see them. When I paid my printing bill I noticed each page cost ten cents per book! Strangely, I felt secure in my publishing decisions with the dimes as my reassurance.

When I finally had the cherished book in my hands I flew to England to speak to the townspeople of Petworth. It was an emotional week. When I took my seat on the plane, my eyes spotted a dime on the floor in front of me. The planes are cleaned before loading passengers, right? But I knew nobody could tidy away my special dimes. As I leaned back in my seat, I began to relax. I could feel John Baron on that plane, escorting me back to a land where we had lived and loved centuries ago. I was blessed in knowing I was never alone.

I loved sharing these experiences with Jill who understood completely. She watched as my synchronicity continued to steer me in torrents on my new research for my past life in the Holocaust. She dubbed me the synchronicity queen.

One day, I went to the library to search for books about reincarnation. I stumbled across an old book titled *Beyond the Ashes*, by Rabbi Yonassan Gershom. The book was about the victims of the Holocaust who are reincarnating, as the Rabbi wrote, *en masse*. My body trembled with the familiar wave of awe and love. Synchronicity, like my dimes, always felt like magic, and I had just been gifted again.

I immediately checked out the book and hurried to

my car. Wow! I hadn't thought of others reincarnating from the ashes of the death camps. Of course, millions of Jews died and if one reincarnated many probably wanted another trip to earth. My God, I was not alone!

I devoured the book in one sitting and felt a heavy veil lifting as if the rabbi had written it especially for me. The book described my entire life. Rabbi Gershom counselled many people who claimed to have memories of the Holocaust. He compared accounts with other analysts and hypnotherapists and noted a common thread through their stories.

He observed that returned victims were born mostly between 1947 and 1953. I came along on February 12, 1953. Most were of Scandinavian descent. Many were non-Jews and knew nothing of Judaism, yet sustained tastes or habits relating to their Jewish past life. Many experienced olfactory or scent recognition, a psychic experience connecting them to their Jewish past in the Holocaust.

The rabbi went on to say that some returnees read magazines and books from back to front, the way Hebrew books are bound.

"Yes, I do that!" I shouted to my quiet apartment. "I read magazines from back to front." I fit into every category, verifying what my inner self already knew. *I was a reincarnated Jew.*

In my excitement I quickly wrote the Rabbi an e-mail telling him that I, too, read magazines backwards. Later I was angry with myself for writing such a trite note. I should have shared, that since age ten, I remembered the camps, the music, the choking smells. I wanted to tell him I perfectly fit his profile of a reincarnated Holocaust victim. Silly of me not to mention the important details. Instead, I only mentioned reading magazines from back to front as Hebrew books are bound, back to front. No wonder the rabbi never replied.

Fifteen minutes after sending the e-mail I felt restless, and walked aimlessly down Revelstoke's main street ending up in the bookstore. It was a busy Saturday afternoon and my favorite clerk Wenche (pronounced Vanka) was busy with a customer.

As I perused the new releases Wenche finished with her sale and bounced over with her bubbly personality.

"Jewelle, would you like a free book?" she asked.

"Sure," I replied.

She disappeared into the store's office returning with a book, placing it in my hands. It was really the book's guts because the cover was gone.

"We tore the cover off this book because it was bound incorrectly. We can't sell it, so you can have it for free," she said. "It's weird. It was bound backwards. You would have to read it from back to front."

I began shaking and scanned the pages. The book was about angels. I read the book's acknowledgements and gasped. The author thanked Jan Tober and Lee Carroll, authors of *The Indigo Children*. Jan Tober is my friend and had endorsed the back cover of my own book *All You Need Is Love*.

Wenche watched my shaking hands with curiosity. I sputtered out my story about my past life in the Holocaust, finding the rabbi's book, and now coincidentally this backwards bound book, was being plopped in my hands.

"I have shivers," Wenche laughed nervously.

"What's the title of the book?"

We searched the pages together. *Divine Guidance* by Doreen Virtue. My heart skipped a beat.

"*Divine Guidance*. You are being guided," Wenche said, and repeated, "Guided."

Two days after reading Doreen Virtue's backwards bound book, I returned to the bookstore.

"Why did you give the book to me?" I asked Wenche. She had never given me a book before.

"You just happened to come into the store at the perfect time, so you got the book."

"Were any other copies of *Divine Guidance* damaged?" I asked.

"No," she replied, "We received three copies and only one was spoiled. The copy I gave you."

"I published my first book myself," I said, "Can you imagine the disaster, if thousands of copies of *Divine Guidance* were bound backwards?"

Wenche called the book's distributor in Vancouver but they had no calls or returns concerning *Divine Guidance* or complaints of improper binding. As far as Wenche could determine, only one copy of *Divine Guidance* was bound backwards, and that imprint, published in the United States, ended up in my hands in tiny Revelstoke, fifteen minutes after writing to the rabbi about reading magazines from back to front.

Early the next morning, as CBC Radio hummed in the background, I watched the sun peek over a mountain top. I gulped caffeine as I struggled to awaken for another working day.

Suddenly, I was jolted from my morning fog. Just before the news, *The Blue Danube* began to play—the beautiful Strauss waltz that, for me, conjures a bittersweet memory of past life and death. I had never heard *The Blue Danube* played on this radio station and now it was serenading me on the morning after my *Divine Guidance* experience. How could I deny this astonishing and persistent guidance into a past existence? Suddenly I was scared out of my mind. I switched off the radio before the music faded.

# FIVE

As TIME PASSED I CONTINUED TO AMBLE along the path laid out before me. One day Gertie came to mind, a woman whom I met in a genealogy group years ago. Back then I was learning to search for ancient family records in England. While the rest of the group searched their family trees, I searched for records of my past life. Gertie had moved to Canada from Germany after the war and was a teacher's assistant for children with learning disabilities. I was impressed and surprised when once she went to great lengths to find me a map I needed and even when I left the group I always remembered her kindness.

I located Gertie and we set a time to meet the next week although it made my stomach ache to think about it. She had lived through the hideous *World War II* era and I was afraid to hear her memories yet I *had* to know. I wished my sister Konni was here; I knew she would have some insight into this Holocaust life.

Konni was on my mind, too, when I bought a new cell phone and saw strange symbols start popping up on the display screen just as they did when I spoke to Konni on my regular phone. With symbols still on my phone's call display I quickly drove to the store and showed the girl who sold me the phone.

"I've never seen this before," she said, examining the backwards Ls, dots, and scribbles.

"I really need to know what these symbols mean," I pleaded. She looked at me cautiously. "Do you think it's the phone, or you?"

I laughed. I certainly wished I knew. She gave me the phone number of the head office.

"Maybe one of their technicians can help," she offered. But the phone company was no help.

"Ma'am you must have dropped the phone in water," the expert suggested.

No, I hadn't dropped the phone in water. I knew the strange symbols were not your normal phone problem. It was another clue of some kind. But what? I hung up in frustration. I felt out of sorts again. Different thoughts cascaded through my mind. I should throw the phone away, discard the poem, and cancel my visit with Gertie. But instead I called my pal Ros.

Our expensive, overseas phone calls were reserved for special occasions so she was surprised to hear from me. Usually Ros was delighted to chat, but today she sounded agitated.

"I received your last letter, and there's a reason I haven't answered. The letter was lovely but your P.S. ruined the whole letter. I felt like you threw cold water on me. I'm talking about your plans to investigate a past life in Germany or wherever those horrid camps are. Please don't tell me about it. I don't want to hear one word about it. I ripped your letter into a million pieces. It's going to ruin our friendship if you start poking around over there. I don't want it to come between us."

"Ros, I promise it won't ruin our friendship." After I hung up I thought, *why would it ruin our friendship for God's sake?* I loved her. She was like a sister. Ros had helped me for ten years as I unearthed my past life in Petworth. Her voice was so panicked that, I was glad I hadn't told her about the channeled poem. I would have to deal with Ros later but now it was time to interview Gertie.

Gertie's hair was still a natural blonde and I stared into her blue eyes as she invited me to sit on her living room couch before a cozy pot of tea. As she served the warm drink with a splash of milk I told her about my search for information about war-torn Germany.

"I don't want to offend you, Gertie," I gently explained. "I know it was a frightening time in your home country. If it's too hard to share, I will understand."

To my great delight Gertie was pleased to reveal the details, and forgetting her tea she straightened in her chair and began.

"We lived in Cologne," Gertie said in her heavy German accent. "My first childhood memories are of nightly bombings, and sleeping in the cellar. I was only a child, but I remember it was like cloak and dagger days. The walls had ears, you couldn't trust anyone, not your brother, your cousin, not even your children."

"Why not the children?" I asked.

"I belonged to the *Hitler's Youth Movement*. All young people were forced to join. It was *mandatory* but my mother and father invented all kinds of excuses for us to miss some of the *Hitler Youth* meetings. If a child attended one of those meetings and unwittingly revealed his parent's anti-Nazi views, it was grounds for punishment. That's how the Nazis kept control; prohibiting the right to free speech—at the same time, the *Hitler Youth* group was brainwashing the young people with Nazi propaganda."

"Did you know any Jews?" I asked quietly.

"I recall a family from down the street who was sent away. We never saw them again. We were told they were sent to a work camp. I also remember people on the streets with yellow stars on their jackets. We, as a people, had no idea until after the war of the death camps.

"We lived in constant fear. We were afraid of everything. Of saying the wrong remark to the wrong person, afraid of a knock on the door in the middle of the night. My father was forced to join the German army. The army was different from the SS. The SS were special forces of cruel men in black uniforms. My cousin was sent to a concentration camp, for his views. He *did* return after the war, but he was a changed man."

"Did you always live in Cologne?"

"No, we moved to the country, and life was a bit easier, but we were still hungry and existed on food rations and extra provisions bought on the black market. In the village, Russian soldiers from a nearby prisoner-of-war camp worked in the fields by our house during the day. People used to say the Russians were horrible, but that wasn't true. They showed us photos of their families, and played cards at mother's kitchen table until curfew time. They were a lovely group of people."

I had to gulp back tears. I didn't want to break down in front of this stoic German woman. I sensed it was wrong to cry. Gertie reminded me of an aunt or mother. Her entire *being* invoked bittersweet emotions in me. She reminded me of a family that loomed in a foggy vision, but the memories wouldn't completely surface for I was afraid to remember.

I rummaged in my bag for my poem, willing my tears to bury themselves. I explained my channeled poem to Gertie, and asked if she could held me translate some of the verses.

"I'll try," she smiled.

She explained to me that the name Heinrich in English is Henry and Greta is Margaret. The poem said these were my parents. Interesting because my father in this life is Henry! I flipped my notebook back to the poem and read her the next line, *"Katarina, my love, your name is the same."*

"Katarina is Katherine."

Katherine was my name in my Petworth life, and Katarina was a name I saw once in a regression, in another life in Germany in the 1800s. Yes, the clues could certainly be found in my current life as John Baron had said.

"One more line, *Black bread only to eat*."

"I would think black bread means dark rye," she said.

I suddenly saw, in my mind's eye, the scene from the book as a child—marmalade showering over the concentration camp fence. In later years it puzzled me why expensive marmalade would be thrown to masses of prisoners.

Gertie laughed, "That's pronounced mar-ma-LAD. It means jam. Probably made cheaply from beet juice."

As we parted, Gertie said softly, " I have spent my whole adult life working through the shame of the war. Humiliation for coming from a race who would do these horrific things."

As I drove home, I contemplated that innocent young girl from Cologne, Germany. She carried the dishonor of the Holocaust her entire life while the real savages, the Nazis, probably felt nothing, and lost not one minute of sleep.

# SIX

THE NEXT DAY, I went for a long walk in the rain. The rhythmic patter of rain drops on my umbrella seemed to beat out a line from my poem, *We danced to the music, light on our feet.* I spun on my heels and headed downtown to the music shop and bought a CD of Johann Strauss waltzes. It was years since I had listened to the bittersweet music.

Waltzes make me think of John Baron. They also harkened back to Patrick White, a former lover from my current life. The last time I saw Patrick we danced.

When I met him at age sixteen, Patrick was a complex young man—the *James Dean* of Revelstoke. He was wild and tough, sensitive and shy. He was brilliant yet ended up in court many times. He acted as his own lawyer, his brightness saving his hide. Yet, once free, he turned around and raised Hell again. I was dangerously in love with him. He rarely attended school but earned straight As. And, although he was no angel, Patrick aspired to be a Catholic priest. I wonder where his future would have led him if he lived. His glow was snuffed out in an auto accident at age twenty-three.

It took me years to heal after his death. A past life regression was the key, and while under hypnosis, I

JEWELLE ST. JAMES

spoke with him. He said we shared a past life in the Black Forest region of Germany in the 1800s. We both died young. My name was Katarina.

I recall those early days, reeling from Patrick's death. His name would appear in odd places, and I often saw a young man who dressed and looked exactly like him, wandering the streets.

I read how departed spirits often try to communicate with the living to tackle unresolved issues from their early life. When I wrote *All You Need Is Love*, I stood at his headstone in the graveyard asking for permission to write about him. I felt a bit foolish talking to air, and Patrick was dead silent.

As I returned to my car, a loud and clear thought filled my mind. I jerked to attention. *If you hear 'Crazy Love' by Van Morrison, you know its okay to write about me.* I really doubted my sanity at that point and yet within the hour *Crazy Love* blazed from the radio. Five years passed (yes I counted) before I heard it play again.

No *Crazy Love* this night, however. I lit a candle and sat quietly before pressing *play* on the CD player. The crystal clear *Blue Danube* waltz began and a heart-breaking rush washed over me. I visualized myself dancing in someone's arms, and then I saw *Ros!* She was watching me from a distance. I began to sob. *Ros was there, Ros was there*, pounded in my head. But where were we? A camp, yes, but which facility?

I spent the next week researching and learned that most of the concentration and death camps were in Poland. This was news to me. I assumed they were all in

Germany. Wow! I was missing basic history. The number of camps staggered me. Hundreds were scattered throughout Europe. The names swam before my eyes.

I read some of their names aloud, trying to allow each name to resonate in my subconscious mind. Dachau in Germany? Treblinka or Auschwitz in Poland? Auschwitz was all too familiar. Like the rest of the world, I knew of the atrocious camp. But that was the only name that echoed from within. Auschwitz stabbed through my soul like a dagger. Fragments of memory were all I could grasp. Dancing, Ros, *The Blue Danube*, terror. So much terror that Ros herself had freaked out about the concentration camps when she read the P.S. to my letter.

I began an Internet search. I can't remember how long I searched Auschwitz before I came across these haunting words. *In the distance violins were playing "The Blue Danube." It was intended to calm the Jews going inside the bath-house—except it wasn't a bath-house, it was a crematorium.*

I was like a zombie on a mission, allowing the Internet to take me places I didn't want to go. I read more. *There were six orchestras at Auschwitz and Auschwitz-Birkenau. The music played while the prisoners marched off to work in the morning and marched back at night. The Nazis had a liking for about twelve songs in particular and demanded these tunes be played over and over—two of those being* The Blue Danube *and* Rosamund.

My mouth hung open as I recalled once, Ros pronouncing her name—Ros-a-mund!

John Baron *said* I would find clues to my past existence in my current life. I was aghast.

Then more clarification came straight from the *Nuremberg Trials* transcripts. Waves of horror washed over me. I knew I danced while children were murdered. I feel sick to share this with you, but I remember I danced with a guard whom I loved. We were alone with the music while the officers were busy with the problem of screaming children.

I forced myself to stay at my computer screen and read.

*It was a music camouflage. All we could hear were the screams and we could see the pile of smoke coming out of the crematoriums, and we also used some sort of camouflage—that was in 1944—that was when the Hungarian Jews arrived—we used a music camouflage.*

*At the time the children were burned on big piles of wood. The crematoriums were not working at the time, and therefore, the people were just burned in open fields, and also the children were burned among them. Children were crying helplessly and that is why the camp administrator ordered that an orchestra be made by one hundred inmates, and should play. They played very loud all the time. They played* The Blue Danube *so even the people in the city of Auschwitz (Oswiecim) could not hear the screams.*

*Without the music, the townspeople would have heard the screams of horror; they would have been horrible screams. The people two kilometers from there could even hear those* screams, namely those that came from the transports of children.

The children were separated from their parents, and then put in the Section Three camp. Maybe the number of children were in the thousands.

And then, one special day, they started burning them to death. The gas chambers at the time were out of order, at least one of them was out of order, namely, the one near the crematorium; it was destroyed by the mutiny in a special commandos in August, 1944. The other three gas chambers were full of adults and therefore the children were not gassed, but burned alive.

When one of the SS people sort of had pity on one of the children he took the child and beat the head against a stone first before putting it on a pile of fire and wood so that the child lost consciousness. However the regular way they did it was by just throwing the children on the pile. They used to put a sheet of wood, then the whole thing was sprinkled with gasoline, then wood again, and gasoline, and wood, and gasoline—and then people were placed there. Therefore the whole thing lit.

Question: And what time period of time did that occur Heir Bielski?

Answer: The children you mean?

Question: Yes.

Answer: That was during those three months when most of the Hungarian transports came in; June, July, August 1944. However, what I mentioned about the orchestra was around the end of August. Several thousands were burned to death, alive.

I stumbled away from the computer screen, feeling sick, like I would vomit. The years of *The Blue Danube* made sense. Katarina had danced while children died. I am so ashamed.

# SEVEN

As TIME PROGRESSED I recalled other perplexing memories that seemed to tie me to Germany. When I was married, a German salesman came to our house with an estimate for a new roof. The man's accent irritated me so much, I gestured to my husband to follow me to the kitchen.

"Get him out of here, *now!*" I hissed. I don't know how Bob managed to escort the man out the door, but within minutes he was gone. We did get the roof, but fortunately, never saw the salesman again.

Paradoxically, a German man attended my cousin's wedding. His sister-in-law was marrying my cousin, and he flew over from Germany for the celebration. I recalled teasing him about his German smile.

He laughed and asked, "What does ziss mean, ziss German smile?"

Later I asked myself the same question. Yes, Jewelle, what *did* that mean? Somehow his accent didn't affect me, but I seemed to recognize and like his smile.

It was time to take a giant step I was avoiding. I called Maggy Davidson who owns a beautiful book and spiritual store in a nearby town. I knew she also did past life regressions in a room at the back of her store. In a shaky voice, I made an appointment to undergo a past life regression. I was surprised that I finally had the nerve. Well, I was still afraid, but I craved more answers. The hypnotic process was not foreign to me. I experienced my first regression in the early 1980s when seeking my past life in the 17TH Century so I knew what to expect, to a point.

A regression to the Holocaust era loomed in my mind for years, but was always too formidable to face. Now I had found the courage to set an appointment. But, I was still scared.

I asked my co-worker Tanya to drive me to Salmon Arm. The regression would leave me in a hazy state of mind, and I knew I would need a driver to transport me home. Besides, I didn't want to be alone. Tanya was a warm-hearted soul, and I felt safe in her company.

On a warm spring day we arrived in Salmon Arm, a town snuggled close to the shore of the Shuswap Lake. Tanya was oblivious to past life regressions so she dropped me off at the bakery next to Maggy's store and agreed to meet back at the bakery in two hours. I had fifteen minutes to spare before my appointment so I sat in the bakery trying to center myself with calm thoughts.

Finally, the time came. I entered Maggy's store and gazed about. I felt at ease in the large shop filled with glittering crystals, incense, cards, CDs, and books. I was grateful for the brightness and soothing background music.

Maggy greeted me warmly and showed me to the room behind her office. The space was small, yet tastefully decorated. Again, soothing music played as she pointed to a tall, narrow massage table with crisp sheets, a comfortable pillow and a light blanket. I was grateful for the blanket as my body usually chills during a regression.

Maggy sat at a small table that angled behind the bed and explained the entire process for taking me back in time. Her soft, kindly voice consoled me as she quietly switched off the music and began the relaxing exercises. As my muscles and heart rate slacked and I entered an altered state of consciousness, my fear melted away.

"Picture yourself in an elevator," Maggy purred.

I immediately visualized myself with one of my clients in an elevator I rode nearly every day at work. This is easy, I thought.

"Choose a floor where you want to alight," Maggy said.

I chose the twelfth floor.

"The door is opening, so you may depart from the elevator."

As I stepped off the elevator, I was no longer mentally in my client's apartment building. Instead, the hallway was panelled with old, faded wood. My stomach sank. A man in uniform was following me! I felt scared, terrified, trapped. I knew I was close to death, but I remained silent, now moving through the hall like lamb to slaughter.

"Where are you?" Maggy asked.

"In a room," I murmured. "Empty, except for a desk, chair and light bulb hanging from a cord."

"What are you wearing?"

I was puzzled. I wore no real clothes, just rags tied together. I barely had a body. I was skin and bones, literally.

"What are you wearing on your feet?"

I looked down. Again I was puzzled. They weren't shoes, but random bits of unidentifiable material tied up with bits of string.

"How old are you?"

"Nineteen."

"Are you alone?"

"A man is here."

"Describe the man."

"He's wearing a uniform —a green-grey uniform." The attire was immaculate, with not a wrinkle or a smudge of dirt. I felt frustrated as I struggled to see his face. He was tall. The brim of his hat slanted over his eyes and shielded his upper face as if he was hiding his identity. This was my observation as Jewelle, for my *other* self wasn't aware of these minute subtle details. I knew I was starving, actually beyond hunger, to the point where my brain was fuzzy and numb.

"What name does the officer call you?" Maggy coached.

"*JUDE*. He calls me Jude—Jew. I have no name, no identity."

"Are you Jewish?" Maggy asked.

"Mother is Jewish. Papa is not."

"What's happening in the room?" Maggy gently asked.

Although I could hear Maggy's voice, my only reality was the barren room with the stark light bulb, and the feeling of utter hopelessness. The guard began lashing the desk with a riding whip. He was screaming, it sounded like ous, ous, ous. *I was detached from my situation. I was a shell of a person in mind and body with no emotions other than a knowing—death was minutes away.*

"He wants information about my father," I share, my voice quaking. "My father knew where the printing press was. Papa was part of a large organization and was sent away a long time ago. Or it seemed like a long time ago."

"What organization?" I heard Maggy ask.

I didn't know if I could trust Maggy. It was secret. I was forbidden to talk about my father's escapades. I felt implanted in the 1940s. 2005 did not exist yet. Even though I lay on the bed in the serene room, my inner self was held hostage in a Nazi prison camp interrogation room.

"Papa has been gone a long time now and our family was part of the underground resistance," I blurted out.

"What did the organization do?" Maggie asked.

"We worked at night distributing flyers/papers, with instructions on how others could resist, and how our group could help the people. To save one person in ten thousand was a victory, Papa would say. We moved people from home to home, and later we resisted through the printed word. We dropped small parcels of newspapers, like flyers, at drop off points. Others would pick up the papers and distribute them. The printing press was in a cellar."

I suddenly heard Papa's voice.

*"Remember, my daughter, the written word is your strongest weapon. We, and no one, can win against the Nazis—but remember my child, our strength comes from the written word."*

I was shaking; tears flowed down my cheeks as I *felt* my father's message. Printing the written word was the very essence of Papa. Buried deep in my soul for decades, the memories of his life in publishing now sprang forth, reuniting me with my own past. The powerful reunion wracked my body with emotion.

As Maggy gently guided me back to the interrogation room, Papa's spirit vanished and I was again left alone with the guard.

"What year is it?" Maggie asked.

"1944."

I could see the officer once again. He was whipping the table, and I seemed to be watching the scene from the ceiling. Strangely, he continued screaming at me as if it was for the benefit of someone outside the door for he never laid a finger on me. *"Ver* is the printing press?" he demanded.

Before I could answer he pulled out his gun and shot

me once in my stomach. I crumpled to the floor and died instantly. From my ceiling vantage point I watched as my bleeding body was dragged out of the room.

I heard Maggy's voice again. She suggested we explore more lives, seeking a common thread between this life and possibly others. I felt myself travelling down an endless hallway or tunnel. I could see lives on both sides, yet I groggily said, "No. No more lives." Maggy took me through a healing mediation but honestly I ignored her words. Awake again, I left the quiet room and returned to the bakery next door to wait for Tanya. I had tea. My stomach hurt.

When Tanya joined me for a pastry I told her about the shooting and how I was still feeling the pain in my abdomen.

She looked at me a bit puzzled. "You don't believe this do you?"

I smiled and dropped the subject. As she consumed her tartlet, I thought of Papa. My mind was still in the 1940s. I longed to tell him, through time and space that I understood about the written word. I am an author in this life, but most importantly I publish my books myself. "My soul remembers, Papa," I said in my mind. I prayed he could hear my thoughts. I now understood why I never tried to land a publisher. Deep in my soul I indeed remembered and understood his message. I understood that publishing, printing and valuing the written word was the essence of who our family *was*.

# EIGHT

MY PAST LIFE REGRESSION AS A JEW was like testing the water. It reminded me of my childhood days swimming in the lake. We would slowly enter the water splashing our arms to test the temperature, then plunge in even if the water was cold. My past life regression now immersed me in the depth of time, chills and all.

More memories floated to the surface. I remembered being sixteen, in 1969, and watching the Vietnam War demonstrations on television. Angry zealous teenagers by the thousands protested the war with such vigor the world was forced to absorb the message. America, had never seen such demonstration. A generation of *flower children* defying authority, demanding peace.

In a flash of insight, I knew that these young rebels were reincarnated from *World War II*. The entire peace movement made sense. The flower children remembered war at the soul level, recalling wicked deaths. No way in Hell would they have war again. They risked arrest, riots and even death to validate their innate hatred of violence and longing for peace. It felt like a vision, one I forgot until I read Rabbi Gershom's words about baby boomers reincarnating *en masse.* I was one of them.

I found many others who remembered as well. My friend Jane is a WASP, so we laughed hysterically when we discovered mutual feelings of a Jewish past life.

Jane remembers when she was younger and living in Vancouver. She travelled by bus nearly every day past a temple with a huge Star of David. On every trip she waited to see the beautiful symbol.

"The Star of David has always been precious to me," Jane shared. "If our town had a synagogue I would convert to Judaism. Actually, my soul *is* Jewish."

Jane's story motivated me to reach out to others. Millions were back on earth and I suspected, many remember. After all, the Nazis murdered six million Jews. I sent an e-mail to everyone I knew asking if anyone felt a connection to *World War II.*

My friend Jacky Newcomb is an author in England. She has written four books about angels and spirit communication along with numerous magazine articles plus radio and television appearances. I was excited when she answered my request.

*"It's funny, but I hated watching anything to do with the war or the terrible atrocities against the Jewish people. I have this terrible dread it might be because I had a past life as a German soldier during the war, and that I was one of the terrible people who carried out these crimes. You know, when I was at school, I always found German easy to learn, almost as if I had done it before.*

*Of course, I have no proof of this at all. I often wondered*

*Prisoners standing during a roll call, Buchenwald, Germany, 1938–41. Photo courtesy USHMM.*

*A yellow Star of David badge bearing the German word "Jude" (Jew). Photo courtesy USHMM.*

*The views or opinions expressed in this book and the context in which these images are used do not necessarily reflect the views or policy of, nor imply approval or endorsement by, the United States Holocaust Memorial Museum.*

*why I picked my current life to help and guide people (people write to me from all over the world to discuss their paranormal experiences which often occur during times of grief and distress in their lives.) Because of my work with angels, I am often called "The Angel Lady." It's like I feel the need to pay back by living a life of compassion and working with the higher realms.*

*Although I have been through past life regression several times with hypnosis and relaxation techniques, and even spontaneous past life recall, I have never felt comfortable at looking back at this possible life. Maybe within this lifetime I will never be able to face that possible truth. But then maybe I was never a German soldier at all!"*

My next response also arrived from England in a letter from a lady who wishes to remain anonymous.

She told about her sister, Carrie, who suffered nightmares about her time in Auschwitz during a past life.

"She seems to know things about the Holocaust without ever knowing about it," my friend said. "Carrie even knows some songs they used to sing in the camps to keep up morale."

Another letter came from Sarah Stewart who was born in England and now lives in Alberta, Canada. She wrote:

*When I was five years old, my cousin gave me her green striped dress as a cast off. When my mother wanted me to wear the dress I became hysterical. She insisted and I cried all day. There is even a photograph of me on that day crying my eyes out. I never wore the dress again and that whole incident left a strong impression on me. As a teenager, I saw photographs of people in a concentration camp wearing green striped clothing and I made the connection.*

*Another time, I was taking a drama class and in one exercise, members brought in photos and we had to create a story about them. One young man brought in a photo of a man. He must have been wearing some kind of uniform, I only remember shirt sleeves but no other clues in the photo.*

*I don't know where the idea came from, but I spilled out, "He was a solider who has just put people on the train to a concentration camp."*

*The young man's eyes narrowed, "It's my grandfather, a German who was doing just that." He then declared his grandfather was forced to do it, and thus not responsible. The class disagreed, and he looked distressed.*

*It is rather a comfort to write these things without expecting some rationale or disbelief from someone. I didn't think anyone would understand about the dress incident or the rest of it, so I kept it to myself.*

# NINE

WHILE MANY OF MY PAST LIFE MEMORIES of the Holocaust terrified me, I was fascinated with my papa's connection with the underground. My sister Konni's words twenty years ago resonated in my mind. *Your family was part of an underground movement transporting people out of Germany.* How I wished I could now ask her for more information. Why didn't I tap her source two decades ago?

On my own, I visualized living in a country house with people arriving and departing in the dark of night. Was this image accurate? I needed proof. My past life regression reawakened my interest. When the veil lifted on that life, I actually felt Papa's spirit, so I began to paint a picture of our underground life with the few clues I had.

I sat at my computer with a large mug of hot chocolate and began to search the Internet. Through my studies I discovered the Resistance cunningly hid Jews, smuggled food and medicine, hid families and sabotaged communication lines. My regression information was correct!

Underground journalism began with secret flyers

denouncing Hitler's propaganda, and urged people to defy the regime. Brave warriors like Papa scrounged paper on the black market. With supplies scarce, the resisters cut the paper into smaller sheets to multiply the copies. Resistance information was printed on one side of the document and furtively posted on walls. Within a year, underground publications had a circulation of five to ten thousand.

I deeply admired the bravery of the underground Resistance. I don't know if I could muster such courage myself. I read about two valiant university students, Sophie Scholl and her brother Hans, who started a support group and an underground press called *The White Rose*. Their covert team in Munich produced flyers condemning the Nazi regime and calling for the restoration of democracy. They copied addresses from the telephone directory and sent anonymous leaflets to people all over the country.

One day, Sophie and Hans dropped a stack of flyers in a university square. A janitor spotted them and reported them to the *Gestapo*. They were arrested and days later, they were tried and sentenced to death. This was one of many heart-wrenching stories.

Involvement in the Underground was exceedingly dangerous. Punishment was often on-the-spot shooting and death. Some resisters were immediately condemned to a concentration camp. Obviously, because my family's *profession* was so perilous, I would never find correct records. I had seen in my regression that

Papa was sent away before the rest of the family. I now feel the Nazis probably shot him, but I will never know for certain.

The glaring jeopardy did not halt the brave men and women of the Underground. By the spring of 1944 the underground press boomed, distributing one and a half million clandestine periodicals a month.

One of those newspapers, *Combat*, issued terse instructions.

*Let us recommend to you the utmost caution. Distribute the newspaper as fast as possible. Avoid keeping bundles of it at home for any length of time. Never send a package of papers by mail. Never write any name on a package or newspaper.*

*Friendly readers, gather around us; set up smart cells—we may one day have other things for you to do.*

*One last point, be discreet: do not try to know who makes your newspaper, do not try to find out where it comes from . . . On the other hand, don't forget to have each copy read by a dozen of your friends.*

*Let us not confuse caution and cowardice. Our newspaper is not meant for those who, comfortable ensconced in an armchair, would read it on the sly and then hasten to burn it for the sake of caution.*

As I read the directives, I completely understood Papa's philosophy and his mission. The words were a proud connection to my valiant family, probably the only link I would have. I only knew my parents' first names and all hope was dashed when I read that nobody kept statistics on the publishers and journalists who worked for the underground press. Strict anonymity was essential, and they often used pen names. It is impossible to trace the true identities of these bold rebels.

I re-read *Combats's* announcement. One sentence confused me.

*Friendly readers, gather round us; set up smart cells.*
What were smart cells?

I read my channeled poem again.

*German you were, a Jew as well*
*I was the soldier, you in the cell.*

This one line, *you in the cell,* had always puzzled me for I couldn't imagine myself in my own prison cell. Weren't the cells swarming with prisoners?

My friend Renee is an amazing psychic even if she's shy about it and labels it her *sixth sense*. She's so timid to admit her talent, she even asked that I change her name for this book. I rarely see her, but our souls are bonded. Even when apart for years, we immediately resume our friendship when we reconnect.

One night, Renee e-mailed me. It was great conversing with her again, and our e-mails zipped back and forth. One night, Renee unexpectedly wrote, "Jewelle, can you smell the ink ... the printing press?"

I was stunned.

Renee explained she was having a *sixth sense evening*

and offered to tell me more. I sent her the channeled poem.

"You knew the guard before arriving at the camp," she wrote.

My fingers dashed across the key board. "Tell me more!"

"The guard was really just a boy forced to be a man, shoved into Hitler's army. You knew him during happier times. The guard was shocked when you arrived at the concentration camp, for he didn't know you were Jewish, and he thought you were safe at home."

My regression proved Renee's information of the printing press was correct, but I was unsure if I had known the guard before the prison camp. I needed more proof to see the complete picture.

Renee suggested I read the book *Jackdaws* by Ken Follett about the French Resistance. The book was action packed, absorbing me with every sentence of vigorous fighters, courageous beyond belief.

I was excited when I came across the word *cell*, but not a prison cell. I learned that covert cells were set up within the underground system to limit the damage if a member was captured and interrogated. Members of individual cells only knew the identities of people within their own cell. Cell leaders communicated with other cells controlling the risk of multiple arrests and deaths.

I now understood the line, *I was the soldier, you in the cell.* "It means a resistance cell!" I wanted to shout to the world. I called nearly everyone I knew, and was a bit humbled when everyone, except me, seemed to know about the resistance cells.

"Jewelle, you need to read more spy books," my sister teased.

But I was elated to decipher another line in my poem. Alway the skeptic, I required authentication from outside myself, and I had just found it. I now settled with my inner visions of Papa in a brave underground organization. Sadly, I had to accept that I would never learn the names of the other fearless comrades who battled along side my family.

# TEN

As my daily life as Jewelle St. James, a traveling nurse's aide in Revelstoke, Canada progressed, past life clues continued to accumulate from amazing sources. One day, I was surfing the Internet and landed on a website for Sahar Huneidi, a psychic in London. I perused her site with interest and noted that she is listed as one of the top one hundred psychics in the world. I wrote to her immediately and told her about my past life with the soul of John Lennon. I even wrote an article about the adventure that she featured on her website. She kindly reviewed my book and offered me a free psychic reading. I was thrilled.

For weeks, I waited impatiently for Sahar's taped reading to arrive in the mail. I eagerly slammed the tape into my recorder and settled down to absorb the information. Immediately she observed what she called my overwhelming sadness. That was odd because I didn't feel sad. Certainly I had overcome the pain of my past loss in the 17TH Century. It took two decades to come to terms with that sadness, but ultimately it left me peaceful. Sahar's melodic voice played for a full hour, and the rest of her reading rang true.

I clicked off the recorder. My God, Sahar picked up

on *sadness*. Why out of her lengthy and remarkable reading did that one sentence bother me? I didn't want to explore sadness anymore. I told my daughter Joanne about the analysis.

"Mom, you've always been sad," she said.

Now I felt terrible. Did I raise my children as a sad mother? This sadness bit seemed alien, and now I was annoyed.

Joanne was on a roll, chuckling as she told me I have many weird quirks.

"Mom, every time someone is in distress, you give them water," she reminded me. "If my son cries, you give him a glass of water. You always check the dog's dishes when you visit my house." My daughter Kristy agreed and said they had talked and laughed about this for years.

I was miffed. They were mocking me. I never noticed my water giving habit. Then I thought about it and recalled my training for home health care. Our class was required to spend time in a senior care facility. One afternoon, our teacher told us we could individually choose how to spend our time helping the residents. Some played cards with the oldsters, while others walked with them, sharing long conversations. I gave everyone a drink of water.

Okay, I had to admit, I was a kind of watering machine for animals, children and the elderly. But in my current life, I did not recognize the sadness Sahar detected.

At the time, I had been visiting Mikel and Mila every

Sunday for two years, and we now felt comfortable with each other. One heart-warming day Mila was lucid and happy, which spurred Mikel's jovial mood as well.

The previous week I had begun reading more about concentration camp life. The prisoner's diets consisted mostly of watery soup, watery coffee and black bread. Turns out the black bread wasn't the wonderful pumpernickel or dark rye the German baker described. The bread was mostly sawdust blended with a little flour and served with soup made from rotten turnips and potatoes. This diet, combined with hard labor, murdered thousands of prisoners within weeks of their arrival.

Often the Nazi guards, for *fun*, ordered starving Jews to stand by long tables of delicious food and observe while the *SS* enjoyed sumptuous banquets. The Nazis employed numerous other ways to humiliate and murder Jews. First they mutilated their spirits, and then they killed their bodies. I now understood my present need to nourish others.

I didn't mention any of this to Mikel, but I did ask if he knew about black bread. He laughed, "Ah, that was my first discovery when I left Europe! Black bread is really just brown bread. It's all in the translation. It means the same as what we call brown bread. There are many different brown breads, yes?" I laughed with him. Of course, brown bread. I never would have figured that out.

The mood in the Polish house was light today, perhaps because Mila was mentally alert. I made a pot of tea, and Mikel brought out a tin of cookies. We began talking about the jobs we had worked at through the years.

Mila's favorite job was a cook. She asked about my job that brought me to her house.

"Oh," I answered vaguely, "I have good and bad days, just like good and bad jobs."

"I understand bad jobs," Mila said. "Working in the factory for the Germans. I hated it."

"Why didn't you quit?" I asked, biting a cookie.

"Because the Nazis would have shot my family."

I coughed, the cookie now stuck in my throat. After everything I'd read and seen in regression, I was still far from truly understanding the horrors these people had lived.

It was shortly after hearing about Mila's work place horror that I decided I must return to my roots. I didn't want to, but knew I *had* to visit Auschwitz and experience it in person.

I told my friend Renee about my plans and she offered to accompany me on the trip.

"Jewelle, I'm frightened, you can't go there by yourself," she said. Yet I couldn't ask Renee, or any friend, or even my daughters to shoulder my burden if I broke down. Instead, I trusted my sister, Korinn, to escort me and was relieved when she said yes.

We booked a flight for November, 2005. I had six months to steel myself. I knew the horrors of the Holocaust, and some facts about the Underground and the Jews, but I needed to emotionally prep for my visit.

Little did I realize that nothing can prepare you for Auschwitz.

I busied myself with the practical side of the trip, searching the Internet for tourism websites about Auschwitz. I nearly fell off my chair. A Scottish professor wrote a book called *Dark Tourism*, about macabre sites around the world, including Auschwitz. The author's name is Professor John Lennon. How strange is that?

I spent the next three months trying to sabotage my trip on a subconscious level. I tried to convince myself that I could understand my past without actually traveling there. I could sit home in comfy Canada watching the snow fall and read about Auschwitz on the Internet. But in the end, I wasn't fooling myself.

"We don't have to go to Poland," I told Korinn. "You probably don't want to." But she was keen for the Poland trip.

I considered just staying in England and showing off Petworth to my sister. I was now comfortable with that past life. But as synchronicity would have it, Ros said she would be away on a holiday during that time. I finally accepted that we were going to Poland.

An old friend, Pat, whom I rarely hear from called, and I told her about my trip to Poland.

"You better take your woollies," she said.

"What do you mean?" I laughed.

"There's nothing worse than the cold, and there's no place colder than Poland."

Her words settled over my soul like an ominous cloak.

# Eleven

I LAY IN BED, STILL AWAKE, as the sky lightened over our Krakow bed and breakfast.

Korinn squirmed awake from her slumber and slowly opened her eyes, squinting in my direction. "You awake?"

"Yes," I mumbled. Actually, I had never slept. There would be plenty of time for rest after today, my second visit to Auschwitz. Would it be easier with Korinn? The death camp was no longer a frightening unknown. But would I break down with my sister there?

Korinn bounded out of bed to take the first shower. I knew the excursion was a sightseeing adventure for her—it was much more than that for me. We were dressed and fed by nine o'clock and proceeded down to the street to await a bus or van. Instead, a lady in a dinky car picked us up. Forget the tour bus, not in November anyway, it was just we three on a tour of Auschwitz.

An icy rain slashed the dark streets as we slowly made our way out of the Russian-looking city. The tour lady struggled with English, which we appreciated, and instead of the typical tourist blurb, she told us a bit about her life. "My first husband was a soccer player," she said, "We lived in Pennsylvania for three years. Do you live near there?"

"No," Korinn said, "we live in the far west of Canada."

"Do you miss living in the U.S.?" I asked, thinking Poland and the U.S. were worlds apart.

"I miss, how do you say? . . . malls. I miss the malls," she said, and we all laughed.

I relaxed on the drive as we enjoyed a personal glimpse of life in Poland, but it ended much too quickly as our guide dropped us at *Auschwitz One*.

"You will now connect with a tour already in progress," she directed and bid us farewell.

Pulling my coat tighter around my neck for warmth, Korinn and I entered the ominous gate. I immediately noticed a sign I had missed yesterday. *Children under the age of fourteen are not allowed to tour Auschwitz.* Thank God! It really was too sickening for any age.

Our new guide slapped red stickers on each of our coats.

"We have several groups touring today," explained the thick accent. "I don't want to lose anyone."

After ten minutes I hated being herded like cattle, and the tour guide lost Korinn and I as we headed out on our own. I was, once again, awash in my own strong memories and feelings, unable to talk. I ripped the red sticker off my coat. It felt like a badge and I refused to be identified. Especially not here.

"Do you want to be alone?" Korinn asked, sensing my sombre mood. We agreed to separate and experience Auschwitz in our own way. I was relieved to be alone

82                                    JEWELLE ST. JAMES

again and began to walk among the large red-brick buildings. Once more, time stood still.

Today I felt defiant compared to yesterday's sadness. Just one day before I had actually been afraid to touch the barbed wire fence, as though it would jolt me with electricity. Today I touched it. I delighted in standing behind a Nazi sign that declared HALT. I will stand wherever I want, you bastards, I wanted to shout.

Yet the black watchtowers were eerily empty and I was aware that the Nazis were not looming guard. Where were they? I felt they *must* be present, but were ignoring the commotion.

I crossed paths with Korinn several times and was glad for her presence. Knowing she was only a few steps away comforted me, even though I was alone with my thoughts.

I omitted the *Killing Wall*, but entered one of the barracks where an enormous glass cannister was displayed, filled with human ash. The sight alarmed me. Suddenly I heard soothing words in my mind, *Just go, just walk, we will guide you.* My guardian was true to his word. As I entered each building it was empty even though hundreds of tourists explored the barracks right next door. I was grateful for the privacy to think.

Korinn and I eventually met up and visited a barrack dedicated to the Jews. Again tourists milled outside, but the building we entered remained vacant. I showed Korinn the Hebrew lettering—the same as the symbols on my cell phone. How in Hell did that happen? I knew it was the unseen yet powerful force steering my life. I will never truly understand how Hebrew letters could appear on my phone's call display for three years.

Korinn disappeared into the buildings's bowels, as I sat in a dark, empty room. Candles twinkled and I noticed a button to play a song. My gloved finger touched it shakily which ignited haunting music. Weary eyes closed and I allowed a cantor's voice singing the mourner's *Kaddish*, the Hebrew prayer for the dead, to sweep me back through the centuries.

Later, climbing to the second floor, the building was still deserted. Gigantic photos captured Jews being tortured, and suddenly an intense claustrophobia enveloped me. My rubbery legs carried me to the wooden staircase and I hastened down. I found Korinn outside and vowed to stick by her side.

"I've been to the gas chambers," Korinn told me. "It's right next door to the interrogation rooms where they took the resistance prisoners. Would you like to see that?"

Although still unsteady, I knew I should see it. I knew that if I saw those rooms, as I did in my regression, I would recognize them, but the building with the interrogation rooms was torn down, only its foundations remained.

The gas chambers were haunting. A teenage girl stood at the back of the room with her scarf stuffed against her mouth. Her eyes spoke volumes as she stood waiting for her teacher and classmates. The windows of the gas chambers are open to the fresh air, and yet the scent of chlorine permeates the air.

When the visit was finally over, we found our driver who transported us the two miles to Auschwitz-Birkenau where only twenty-four hours before I had entered the death camp with a group of Jews. Birkenau was as bleak and barren as yesterday. I felt jumpy and quickly turned sensing an angry German Shepherd behind us, but it was only a group of tourists. Suddenly I heard wild barking for real. It's from that town in the distance, I scolded myself. Damn! I wish I could get a grip on myself. I also couldn't help wondering who would want to live with Auschwitz-Birkenau in their back yard.

As it did the day before, the sun descended early and it was time to leave. I panicked. I was afraid to leave!

"I need a minute," I told Korinn and the guide. As they bundled into the car I stood on the same railway tracks that had transported Jews here from all over Europe, sixty years ago. I gazed across the empty fields and tried to say goodbye. I didn't want to leave, and I couldn't say good-bye.

"But nothing is here. My people are gone," I whispered.

Tears flowed as the car crunched out of the parking lot. I felt I was abandoning my roots, and yet in a powerful way, I was also reclaiming my soul.

# TWELVE

THE DRIVE BACK TO KRAKOW passed in a blur. That night at dinner, I drank some wine and tried to celebrate my mission accomplished. I had faced down my fear in the former Nazi death camps. At least that is what I told Korinn. But the wine was really to numb my mind.

Strolling back to our B&B after dinner we noticed elderly folk stooped on the cold streets, selling pretzels. I couldn't imagine our seniors in Canada enduring such harsh conditions for a few extra cents. I was attracted to the seniors I saw around Poland, sitting on tram cars or selling wares in the vast outdoor markets. They were the same generation as Mikel and Mila. I knew that behind the wrinkled faces, their minds were alive with memories of the time I had lived and died. How I longed to reminisce with them.

The next morning, after much needed rest, I felt peaceful. Months later I realized that my tranquillity was actually a kind of shock. It was our last full day in Krakow and I wanted to see the Jewish Quarter of the city. When we arrived, I was surprised to find the squares and streets eerily quiet. The haunting atmosphere was so heavy I could have sawed it with a knife. *Schindler's List* was filmed here.

I remembered from my conversations with Mikel that Germany invaded Poland on September first of 1939 and that ignited *World War II*. Looking around the deserted Jewish Quarters of Krakow today, it was hard to imagine that sixty thousand Jews once lived in Krakow. Only a few thousand remain today. The rest were murdered or fled after the war.

Korinn and I decided to part once more. She went shopping for souvenirs, and I found a synagogue to explore. Actually the synagogue was now a museum and I was shaking with excitement to discover more.

Once inside, viewing the various displays, I realized that my knowledge of history was so lacking that I hadn't grasped that Poland was the country most devastated by the war. The Germans intended to not only to rid themselves of Jews, but the Polish race as well. This process of elimination, the Holocaust, was carried out systematically.

The Polish Jews were herded into ghettos and slowly starved to death while cruelly offered some small hope of survival, but most were shot or gassed. In the end, they were transported to Treblinka or Auschwitz along side the Nazi's undesirables such as non-Jewish Poles, Gypsies, homosexuals, Jehovah's Witnesses and Soviet POWs. Many non-Jewish Poles were either transported to Germany and used as slave labor or simply executed. I thought of Mila sent to work in a German factory.

I read this gruesome declaration from Hans Frank, a Nazi leader in Poland: *"If I wanted to put up a poster for every seven Poles shot, the forests of Poland would not suffice to produce the paper for such posters."* Frank was later convicted of war crimes against humanity and sentenced to death.

I learned that the Poles refused to surrender or co-operate despite the ghastliness. The Polish Underground was the largest in Europe. The Jewish Resistance was set up separately to assist Jews in the ghettos. Both organizations attacked the Nazi military machine. But despite their bold rebellions, literally every family in Poland lost members to torture and murder. I finally understood Mila's statement as she waved her hand from her Revelstoke backyard on a sunny day in September, "This best place in the world, this Canada." I now realized where they came from and why their simple life, which to many appeared mundane, was a joyful one as they awakened every morning to a land unscarred by war.

As I perused the museum, I felt at home. I savoured every Hebrew letter, menorah and photo; I breathed in the ambience. I walked by a group of students sitting in chairs as their teacher spoke in Polish, yet I felt I knew every word the teacher said. The bottom line would always be the same. Thousands of Jews who prayed here sixty years ago were gone—slaughtered. I left the building in the same hurry as my rush to explore the synagogue, and waited outside in the bitter cold for Korinn. My friend Pat was right. Poland is a cold place. I needed my woollies. Despite being warmly dressed I was shivering, and we found a Jewish restaurant.

It was like entering a relative's house. A relation

from another life, that is. A welcoming fire burned in the grate. Two Jewish men ran the establishment. We ordered hot chocolate and walnut cake.

*This restaurant is like my auntie's place*—the thought spilled into my mind before I could analyse it. I had a sudden rush of deja-vu. I remembered dreaming of this room years ago. One of those dreams that hovered in my conscience. The dream featured a sparse room with a table, covered with a lace white tablecloth, and was like a long, forgotten home. Now I was sitting in that exact room. A menorah perched on top of a large piano and lace tablecloths covered old-fashioned heavy wooden dining room tables. An enormous black cat lazed on the floor.

An older woman, in a real fur coat, sat at the next table. I longed to talk with her yet I kept silent. We sipped our hot chocolate while I tried to etch every detail of the scene into my mind and memory. One of the owners stoked the fire and I stared at his skullcap, wondering if there were ghosts in his building, for I surely felt spirits.

We ended our day by visiting the *Galicia Jewish Museum*. Again a grim reminder that after eight hundred years of Jews inhabiting Poland, they were annihilated by one madman and his henchmen. My emotional response was so overpowering that I nearly collapsed. It was like a piece of Hell clung to me. Yet in a matter of hours I would be gone, probably never to return, and I needed a symbol to bring home with me.

I tried on a ring with Hebrew letters adorning it.

Again, the letters were like my cell phone symbols. I saw a menorah I *died* to have but my Zlotys were nearly gone. Then I spotted it. A perfect tiny, shining pin—a Star of David! Fifteen Zlotys. I proudly pinned it on my coat beside my Canadian flag pin. Korinn didn't comment when I announced, "I *am* Jewish."

Our last morning dawned and Korinn ran to the old market area for some last minute photos. I needed to reflect, and didn't want to spend my last hours in Krakow as a tourist. My bags were packed. I wrote in my journal.

*While in Auschwitz I reclaimed myself when I dared to touch the once electrical barbed wire fence, and to stand behind the HALT sign. My journey to Auschwitz is complete—I mustered the courage to go, to understand, to feel the sorrow. Germany was my last life's home, but the feelings there are too horrific to visit that country, because Germany would always end up in Auschwitz. We leave Krakow in an hour. I now understand the sadness that lies deep within my soul. I hope with recognition, I can be free.*

# THIRTEEN

I SPENT MY FINAL MOMENTS in Krakow's international airport fidgeting with my watch. At least I thought they were my last moments. "Where is our plane?" I asked Korinn who looked as eager as I to depart Poland. The loud speaker crackled and we both bent an ear to listen.

"Flight ninety-one to London has been cancelled because of weather conditions."

I sucked in a long breath as we joined the other passengers shepherded out of the airport into waiting busses transporting us to a different airport. The bus chugged through a dense fog, but it didn't shroud the road sign announcing *Oswiecim, five miles.* We were back at Auschwitz! One last chance to feel the eerie ambiance, sharpened by the fog. I felt the same sadness as when we left Birkenau. I glanced down at my Star of David pin. The familiar star comforted me.

I slept the rest of the way to London. As we collected our luggage at Gatwick and hailed a taxi, Korinn looked puzzled. "Where is your pin?"

I grabbed my coat lapel in alarm. Somewhere between Krakow and London I lost my precious Star of David! I held back tears as we settled into a small hotel in London. We both missed the charming B&B in Krakow.

As I thought about the pin, I realized it was time to put Poland behind me. I had a new project to occupy my attention. I was booked as a speaker for a paranormal group in London that evening. The speaking engagement was arranged months before, and I wished now we'd gone to Poland *after* my speech.

The spiritual group was an odd assortment of men and women, and met in a large room over a pub in Earl's Court. Korinn wasn't keen on spending seven pounds to hear her sister speak so she went to investigate the nooks and crannies of Westminster.

"I am an avid John Lennon fan," the chairman said and shook my hand warmly. "I eagerly await your speech."

I felt a flash of irritation. People commonly think I knew John Lennon intimately. Yet, my past life love was John *Baron*, not Lennon. I knew his soul three hundred years before John Lennon was even born. I had never met the Beatle, but I smiled at the chairman as the evening began. I felt a bit hazy as I took the microphone and began to speak.

"When John Lennon was shot, it changed my life forever." My words were slow and hesitant. "I grieved for three years before I made a decision to seek help." I was on the brink of tears. I looked at the audience and froze. I was speechless. Finally, I mumbled, "I'm sorry I have just returned from Auschwitz . . . "

Oh my God, I thought with bitterness. This audience doesn't understand this stuff about Auschwitz. But, I didn't care about my past life as Katherine in 17TH Century Sussex. I couldn't even remember it, let alone talk about it. Instead I began telling the group about seeing, for years, the symbols on my cell phone and finally, days ago, while in Auschwitz, I realized they were Hebrew letters. This group was a paranormal group, after all, a safe place to speak of such things.

I went a step further. I told them about seeing my sister's name on the side of a train three days after her death, and how a friend also witnessed Konini's name spray painted on the boxcar. I told them of other spray-painted messages over a four year period that I observed from my apartment window as trains chugged by.

One day while talking on a cordless phone to my friend Sheila, I walked to the window. I had been speaking about my deceased friend Patrick White. Just then a train stopped and on a boxcar directly in my view was a huge spray painted red heart with the words *July 1974* written underneath. I shrieked to Sheila, explaining the dates. July 1974 was the month and year that Patrick died!

"Another time on a summer's day I was about to listen to a taped psychic reading from Therese, a psychic who connects with John Baron, my 17TH century soul mate," I boldly stated. "The exact second I put the tape in the machine to hear communications from John, a train rolled by my window. It was a hot summer afternoon and I went to shut the window so I could hear the tape. I glanced at a passing boxcar and nearly fainted. On the side of the boxcar in big puffy psychedelic letters was the word BARON. What in hell? The train slowly went out of view.

"I ran out of my apartment, to my car, and followed the train. I felt like a crazy woman chasing the train! The locomotive stopped about two blocks away. I jumped out of my car and stood on the sidewalk looking at the letters on the side of the boxcar.

"Yes, it spelled B-A-R-O-N. I drove home in an absolute daze."

Actually, I felt I was in a daze at this moment. Yet the audience seemed interested so I kept talking, pouring out years of messages and signs in my life. This group was used to weird happenings weren't they? I was hoping someone in the group would offer an explanation but no one did. Oh, that's right, I was supposedly the expert. Hmmmm!

"I've had many messages on the side of trains," I continued. "They come in one word or two with clear simple lettering. One day, a nurse called to tell me my dad had fallen in the care home where he lived. He was elderly with health issues and I immediately worried that he would die from this tumble. I tried to calm myself knowing a fall didn't necessarily mean he would die, yet the death thought nagged at me. I wondered if he would live to his birthday at the end of that month, August.

"I was pacing the floor and heard a train. I looked out the window and on the side of one of the boxcars, in large spray painted letters, was written THE END. The trains were my message billboards during the four years in that apartment. I knew this was my memorandum, my dad wouldn't make it. Dad died ten days later."

I continued pouring my heart out to the group, spewing out chunks of my *Divine Guidance* experiences in no planned order. Heck, I'd already blown it as a speaker for *All You Need Is Love*. The chairman wasn't getting his John Lennon fix.

Instead, I told about the dimes that have appeared by the hundreds through the past decade, the weird coincidences. All appearing when I needed an answer, or direction. All showing me I am guided.

"And if I am guided, *you* are guided," I heard my voice say. A place to stop my rambling. It took me two months after my so called speech to realize I was in a major state of trauma that night.

"How did the speech go last night?" Korinn asked me over a cup of Starbucks coffee.

"A disaster! I'm glad you didn't attend because I was embarrassed."

"Everyone falls on their face, on the journey upwards," Korinn said.

"Yeah, sure," I agreed, trying to laugh. I walked to the counter looking for cream. I glanced down to the shiny floor and there was a five-pence coin that looks very similar to our dime.

I smiled. Maybe there was hope.

# FOURTEEN

AFTER THE EXHAUSTING FLIGHT from England, it was heavenly to arrive home to find Revelstoke all dressed up for Christmas with colorful lights and a blanket of fresh-fallen snow. The festivities were in full swing, including our annual Christmas party. While we awaited our dinner and sipped wine, I asked a nurse about Mikel. The elderly Polish fellow was on my mind.

"Oh, Mikel is failing," she said.

I panicked, and my happiness abruptly dimmed. That night I prayed I could see him one more time.

The very next morning, I drove to the care home where he and Mila now lived. I found Mikel in bed. I crept to his bedside and whispered into his ear, "Hi, Mikel."

His lids fluttered open and he looked at me vaguely, his blue eyes no longer twinkling.

"Do you remember me?" I asked.

His brow furrowed, "No."

"I used to come to your house—home care. I'm the worker who always visits England."

"Ah, yes, yes," he smiled faintly.

"Mikel, I just returned from England. I also visited your country, Poland."

The old man wagged his head and struggled to sit up. "You were in Poland? Warsaw?"

"No, Krakow, and Auschwitz."

"Krakow is good place. Was it cold?" Mikel was now alert, yet feeble.

"Very cold," I said, and Mikel chuckled.

"How's Mila?"

"*Young Lady* not doing so good," he said.

I took a deep breath. "Mikel, I had to see you. Remember all the stories you told me about the war? I thought I understood, but now I know I was ignorant. I explored your Poland. I understand. I needed to tell you, I grasp where you came from. I comprehend your stories now. I know the truth."

Mikel began shaking, his sky-colored eyes watering.

I gulped back my own tears. "Do you want some juice?" I soothed holding the straw as he carefully swallowed. The small effort drained him and he looked weary.

"I'm writing a book, Mikel, and I want to include your stories. May I write about you?"

"Yes, yes," he said, and he proudly straightened his rumpled back. "Tell people too, I went to military school." His smile faded slightly as he labored to breathe.

I took his hand. "I will, Mikel, I will tell them."

Mikel struggled to hold back tears. He laid back on his pillow, closed his eyes and whispered, "Thank you, thank you."

No, thank *you* Mikel, I longed to say. Thank *you* for teaching me who you are and where you came from.

Your stories helped me find myself. I know where I came from too. The words went unspoken. I would not make this proud Pole weep in front of a visitor. It was time to leave this wise man his dignity.

I kissed his forehead, "Merry Christmas, Mikel."

"Merry Christmas to you," he mumbled with great effort.

I ran to my car and burst into loud sobs.

\* \* \*

*Mikel passed away shortly before this book was printed.*

\* \* \*

For two months, I dreamed of Auschwitz. My first dream was of *Auschwitz One* with the barracks transformed into murky suburban houses lined with trash bags at the curb. I woke up and immediately knew I had piles of rubbish to clear out of my soul. Every night for weeks, I dreamed of Poland, the concentration camps, or Nazis. My mind was slowly processing the scenes that I couldn't absorb earlier.

Through out this period several people told me about a local Reiki healer named Frieda. One day, I was stunned to hear her name a third time and knew it was synchronicity. I immediately called for an appointment. Perhaps I could speed the healing process and free my dream time.

As I waited several days for the appointment, other issues pressed my mind. Years ago, before I comprehended my Holocaust past life, I played *The*

*Blue Danube* during a meditation. I visualized Ros in a German life with me in a concentration camp. I tucked the information into the recesses of my mind. It felt heavy and negative, so I ignored the vision. Now it cried out for attention.

The connection between my Petworth and Holocaust lives was unexpected and shocking, and now I needed to confront Ros about her part in the story. I was afraid to approach her about it. She did, after all, freak out when I told her I was investigating concentration camps. In fact, I visited her in 2004 with the channeled poem tucked deep in my purse. I was afraid to show it to her.

But now, I knew I must be bold. I mailed her the channeled poem purposely omitting the little scene with her in my mediation - her in the camp with me. I conveniently forgot her fearful reaction to my letter years ago. I needed her true reaction *now*.

I remembered the night, years ago, when I channeled the poem and John Baron said, "*I have something to tell you about Petworth. I'm not sure you can handle it.*"

I was now ready. But was Ros? The letter was already out of my hands and on its way to England.

# FIFTEEN

MY APPOINTMENT WITH FRIEDA finally arrived and I relished her warm, tranquil home with relaxing music in the background. The gentle atmosphere reflected Frieda's demeanor. This was my first experience with Reiki, a form of energy healing my friends talked about. Frieda led me into a special healing room with soft colors and the aroma of burning incense.

*Jews undergoing selection on "the ramp" at Auschwitz, 1944. Visible in the background is the entrance to Birkenau. Some veteran inmates (in stripes) are helping newcomers.* (Yad Vashem Film and Photo Archive)

"I just bought this incense," Frieda said, motioning me to a bed/table. "It's from a Tibetan monastery called *Ash.*"

This startled me for I thought of the ash still choking the ground at Auschwitz.

I laid on the table, unsure what to expect.

"Chinese mystics discovered Reiki energy," Frieda explained. "The energy is transferred to others through attunement. I was attuned in special classes and now tap the energy and let it flow through my fingers into your body. I am only the facilitator, not the healer. Only you can choose to use the energy to heal."

*Me?* I was hoping to have an hour of mindless relaxation while she did the work.

"All you have to do is open your mind to healing," Frieda said softly as I closed my eyes. "Just relax. The Reiki energy will take over."

I gladly unwound and my mind began to drift into what seemed like daydreams. I thought of Patrick's mother who was also named Frieda. When I lived and worked in a seniors care home, Patrick's mother came for tea. It was bittersweet to chat with her about Patrick, and that was when I realized I didn't know much about her.

"Where were you born, Frieda?" I asked.

"India." She smiled, enjoying old memories. "I was the daughter of a British officer and he was stationed in India when I was born. Later my family moved back to my parent's native Sussex."

*Women and children on the Birkenau arrival platform, known as "the ramp," summer, 1944. Prisoners were removed from the deportation trains onto the ramp where they underwent a selection process: some were sent immediately to their deaths, while others were sent to slave labor camps.* (Yad Vashem Film and Photo Archive, both photos)

"Sussex?" I was shocked. "I visit Petworth in West Sussex," I said.

"Oh, my! I attended school for short time in Petworth," Frieda said.

It was a coincidence beyond belief. Petworth is a small town like Revelstoke. My tiny 17TH Century home was connected to Patrick's mother!

My mind reconnected with the Reiki room. Melting snow dripped off Frieda's roof in a rhythmic patter and the sound lulled me into another daydream. I saw an old brown boxcar. I felt danger, a profound feeling of impending doom yet I was confused. The vision expanded in slow motion. Yes, I was standing by a cattle boxcar. *Oh my God, the selection process at Auschwitz!* I knew the truth! I was plucked from the group and allowed to live, to work. I saw one of my grandsons, in my current life, and a tear tumbled down my cheek. He was my little brother in that life. My mother held his delicate hand as they walked away in hollow silence. *Where is Papa?* Then I realized the Nazis had ripped him from our family long before. *Was he dead?* I never heard from him again.

The scene changed, and I glimpsed snippets of our family involved with the resistance movement—people hiding in our house, Papa publishing and distributing resistance information. His bravery led to his death, but I now realized, the underground press didn't sentence my family to Auschwitz, our mother's Jewish faith did. Somehow, Papa disconnected his family from his own involvement with the resistance.

I was sent to Auschwitz as a Jew but my resistance knowledge was later exposed. The guard with the whip was ordered to torture me for this information. Instead, he spared me continued suffering with a

*An elderly man selected for death, 1944. In Birkenau, the elderly were almost immediately sent to the gas chambers.* (Yad Vashem Film and Photo Archive)

JEWELLE ST. JAMES

merciful gunshot to my stomach. Another tear rolled down my cheek as the perception sunk in.

I could now see the stupid sign over the main camp, translated, *Work Shall Set You Free*. It described my current life, all work and no play. When I work, I'm safe. Even if I feel half dead as I carry out my assigned duties, I'm secure.

My cheeks were damp and I was no longer aware of Frieda or her Reiki energy. I was back there—trapped, working, starving, no hope, only a morsel of kindness from the guard. I saw my friend Patti. She was with me at the camp! She, too, lost her family and we became like sisters watching out for one another.

My thoughts flickered from Patti to Patrick, for we were all friends in Revelstoke. Suddenly my body jolted. I saw myself dancing. What an odd couple. Me, thin, bedraggled, bones jutting out, dancing with the guard. The guard was handsome, his uniform immaculate, his high leather boots kicking up dust. It was a hot day in August, the orchestra played in the distance—*The Blue Danube*.

My thoughts floated for a few minutes and then I saw John Baron channeling the poem to me. Only, they weren't John's words. He allowed the guard to feed the information through him, to communicate my past life story! John Baron, my guide and a natural poet, converted the guard's story to a poem. I learned the truth in a flash—the guard was Patrick!

Then I saw Ros. She was there as the guard hauled me away. *Oh my God!* Something about Papa's involvement with the Resistance, information that somehow leaked out. There may be more to the story but the vision ended there. I now knew Patrick had carried out an impossible form of love, killing me to spare me a worse fate.

For weeks after the Reiki treatment I felt light and happy. It ignited visions that filled in the missing blanks of my Holocaust life. I now understood why Patti insisted I take my woollies to Poland. She was there too!

The next week, a letter arrived from Ros. I eagerly ripped it open and read:

*Dear Jewelle,*

*I feel sick !!! I almost cried when I read your poem. It must be true. No one could make this up. As I read it, I felt I knew about it all although I was never moved by the German Nazi camps. I panicked as I read, thinking, "Oh my God. I've been found out." I wanted to vomit. The information in the poem is familiar like I've always known and now YOU know too. It sounds strange and I have no explanation other than this is how I feel.*

Two weeks later, another letter arrived from Ros.

*Dear Jewelle,*

*I still feel ill when I read the poem. Remember when I became cross when you first told me you were searching the concentration camps from your last life? I was worried about you. I know your last book consumed much of your life, and now you were unearthing something worse. I just wanted you to be an ordinary person, like a tourist visiting England yet strangely, I cannot deny I recognize the scene in the poem. As if I alone knew this story and wrote the poem. I also visualize it written on brown parchment paper surrounded by flowers.*

*Love,*

*Ros*

*P.S. One more thing. I feel I was there in that life as a courier . . .*

My God! I hadn't mentioned the resistance movement to Ros. Couriers were part of the Underground; with-

*Auschwitz–Birkenau, 1944. Women and children waiting in a small wooded area near Crematorium IV. A waiting room for the massive numbers to be murdered. Most had no idea of the fate that awaited them. Elderly women, mothers and young children were also sent immediately to the gas chambers.* (Yad Vashem Film and Photo Archive)

(Yad Vashem Film and Photo Archive)

(Yad Vashem Film and Photo Archive)

JEWELLE ST. JAMES

out them, there would be no news, no communications. Her own memories verified mine. Ros *was* there! John's warning before the poem was written, *Petworth, our beautiful Petworth, is not all you think it is. I have something to tell you, I don't know if you can handle it*—now made sense.

In a flash of revelation, I understood the smoke. Whenever I'm in Petworth I smell smoke, and assumed it must be a 1600s memory, since I lived in Petworth at that time. But that was a smoke screen, no pun intended. A cloud of smoke from the crematoria hung constantly over Auschwitz and Auschwitz-Birkenau. I had brought the smoke memory with me to Petworth and smelled it when I was with Ros.

I called Therese for a psychic reading. The gifted medium easily converses with John Baron. I wouldn't tell her a thing, I decided. I wondered if she, or should I say John Baron my guide, would verify my findings?

# Sixteen

Therese's reading was a few minutes away. I settled into my easy chair by the phone and mulled over my journey to reconnect with my past life during the Holocaust. It all started with memories from my childhood, reading the frightening book when I was ten. Who I was had died, but my soul lives on and remembers.

Waiting for the phone to ring, I mulled the myriad of coincidences over the past twenty-five years. My father used to scold me when I lightly shared these daily occurrences. I can still hear his voice. "There is no such thing as a coincidence." While I recognized the enchantment of this seemingly fluke luck, I didn't understand how it happened.

Meeting author Jill Wellington clarified these magical occurrences. "Why do I have so many coincidences in my life?" I asked her.

She told me about a remarkable phenomenon she studied for years called synchronicity or meaningful coincidences. I researched synchronicity on the Internet and learned that a Swiss psychiatrist named Dr. Carl Jung coined the term explaining that our Universe is connected as one. Jill said spiritual forces are working behind the scenes to create the magical coincidences to move us along life's path. Everyone can remember times of synchronicity. It's universal.

So in a way, Dad was right. A coincidence is not a random, lucky occurrence. It has specific meaning and it was time I paid closer attention. Looking back, I now saw the synchronicity that led me to understand my past life in England and now my Holocaust incarnation. Synchronicity always leads us to our destiny if we don't fight it.

The phone rang—it was Therese, and my reading began. Therese's voice was kind and sweet as she opened the reading with a prayer, asking for the highest light, the highest love, and the highest truth.

"Jewelle, I see your recent journey," she began. "Your being is like an egg. Once cracked, a lot of stuff is gushing out."

That's for sure, I thought.

"Your guide is here," Therese said, "John Baron. John sits by an open window. He's writing at his desk, there's a writing table with an ink well, he dips his quill pen in the ink.

"The view from the window looks out on a garden of purple violets. He turns to smile at you. His energy is rich. He writes and says you are doing this together, you are writing partners. He has so, so much love for you. He says he will give me the information you need, Jewelle. Just ask questions, but don't supply the details."

"I need to know about a guard, in my last life, who shot me." Questions packed my mind, and I felt impatient, wanting them all answered at once.

Therese breathed in slowly. "John is like your gatekeeper. He allows the guard to come through with information. I see a marriage of sorts, like a symbolic marriage, united hearts, between you and the guard.

"Ahead of the war, before he was a guard, he was quite young and naive. When you came into the camp it was quite a shock for him because he remembered you. You knew each other before the war, prior to the horrors. I see him as a delivery boy. He came to your home. This may sound odd, but he was a paperboy or delivery boy. That's how you got to know him."

My mind perked. Paperboy? Papa was in the *paper* business, printing newspapers, I wanted to shout. Obviously people would deliver products to our home.

"There was a spark and connection when you first met. He was eighteen and you were fourteen, when you met before the camps."

My heart raced at the revelation. My psychic friend Renee saw the same thing during her *sixth sense* evening!

"John is showing me more. The guard cared for you with extra food, a hug, a dance. These morsels kept you alive, knowing someone cared, for you were ripped from your entire family."

I wanted to cry. I saw my Jewish mother and little brother trudging away in horrified silence, and where was Papa?

"I can feel your loneliness," Therese paused, "Okay, there's something more here. The guard knew your fate and he couldn't take it.

"John is telling me to imagine two people, pressed into a horrendous situation, yet still allied by their profound heart connection. It *seems* you were simple and naive and he was young and confused, but beyond dreadful appearances, you maintained pure love. Yes, even in human horror, love can survive. To understand, you as Jewelle had to put aside your logical mind and search Katarina's heart."

Therese paused, "Did a current friend share that life?"

I jumped. "Ah, yes, my friend Ros reacts to this life, and my research frightened her."

"I want to call her Angelina, so let's call her that. She knew about your connection with the guard, and she was afraid the Nazis would catch you." Therese's voice changed. "Angelina wanted to cry. She was alone after the guard killed you, and she missed you very much. She is afraid of losing you again. Do you understand this?"

I shook my head in amazement. "Oh, my God, yes, she wants me to be an ordinary tourist with her in England and to quit poking around in all this stuff. It annoys her."

"Yes, your search into the Holocaust life is a huge annoyance for her. She tried to warn and mother you. She was also envious of you and the guard who gave you food, yet she also found it despicable because he was one of the guards."

It all rang true.

"Jewelle, I don't mean to offend, but there was an innocence about you in that lifetime, like you could accept the guard's love although he was the enemy."

I had a flash of dancing while the children *burned*.

"You were a little brain dead, with no thoughts, like a walking zombie."

I now understood why at the end I didn't recognize the guard when he hauled me into the room to shoot me. I was already long gone mentally.

"You completely lost your perspective. Angelina/Ros saw this happening and it horrified her."

So that's why Ros freaked out years ago when I mentioned the concentration camps. Of course, she was sickened when I sent her the channeled poem. She felt like she knew the story, because she *was* there.

Her own feelings were true past life memories that mirrored my own memories. *Ros' memories verified my past life.*

I now knew why I returned to Petworth year after year. It wasn't to heal with John Baron, I had already done that. It was to heal with Ros. My God, our inner self is constantly tying to heal our wounded souls.

"John wants to explain," Therese said. "This is the gist of your story—love, everlasting love. The logical mind desires to rule, and whatever the mind sees, like the war, is just logic. But logic has nothing to do with the heart, so underneath the drama of every incarnation, love prevails. John is smiling now. He says, "Love is all there is."

It was a beautiful way to end my reading with Therese, and that last paragraph stuck in my mind. Two days later, I replayed the tape of Therese's reading. I heard her voice purr, "John Baron, your guide is here. John sits at an open window and writes, he turns to smile at you, he's your writing partner—"

I stopped the tape abruptly. My heart recognized the truth. Of course, Papa and John were still with me at the heart level. I remembered hearing Papa's voice at the *Killing Wall* on that snowy November day in Auschwitz. *The written word, my child, remember!* Earthly incarnations don't separate hearts. John *was* Papa, and our love transcends all time whether we are in a body or in spirit. John was helping me to remember and heal!

With that understanding, I knew my search into my past life ending in Poland was over. It is shocking to think I likely spent only a few weeks in the concentration camp, yet that splinter of time haunted my entire being.

I now understood that our lives are all one. Our bodies die but our souls move on in one big life. For me, this discovery was a miracle. Birth and death aren't the challenge. The test is healing the soul.

I now realize that John Baron, Patrick White and Ros, have traveled through many lifetimes with me, linked in love. We all worked in unison to repair the ugly gash left by the Nazi atrocities. Healing that wound to my soul required me to *first* delve back three hundred years where that love began before I could face my life sixty years ago. It took *two* lifetimes to heal in my current life.

I first had to understand my 1600s connection to comprehend and heal the bigger wound— my past life as a Jewish girl, who lost her papa, whose family was murdered, and who left the earth, - shot dead - not even called by her proper name. She died with the word *Jude* ringing in her ears. How could I begin a new life anywhere with this bleeding laceration to my soul?

Yes, my spirit yearned to heal from the second I was born, supplying clues as guideposts. Nine years passed between my murder at Auschwitz and my current incarnation. My first clue was in my own name, *Jew*elle. I emerged into life on February twelfth, the same date the first German Jews were transported to Poland. I was born at forty-one after two——the exact time *World War II* ended. The moment I entered the world, the nurses buzzed because my body was enshrouded with a delicate membrane known as a *caul*. This is a rare occurrence at birth, and mystics believe a baby born in a caul possesses amazing spiritual gifts. For years I felt my spiritually guided search for past lives *was* a curse, but now I understand it is indeed a gift.

In August 1964, at age eleven, I had a severe accident with fire, and I now wonder if I was reenacting the horror felt by Jewish children who died by fire twenty years earlier in August 1944, while I/Katarina danced with the guard. I know logically this was misplaced guilt but did my soul feel the need to be karmically released? I'll never know for sure.

I also understand my soul mate, John Baron, guided me the whole way. And if I am guided, you are too. How many other baby boomers are out there struggling in this modern world to heal the traumas caused by the *Second World War*? How many of our children are injured spirits who died in the *Vietnam War*? How many of us are repeating a thousand past-life scenarios struggling to heal once and for all?

I thought my first book had healed me. But now I know it was just the beginning.

I am a changed person since leaving Auschwitz. I reclaimed my power. People around me notice the change too, and not everyone likes the new me, but for the first time, I *know* who I am, and I missed my authentic self.

I now know my mission in this life is to share my own healing through the written word so that others may recognize themselves and restore their souls too. If you were drawn to this book and related to my story, your soul is urging you to remember. Open your mind to your own innate guidance that is longing to help you heal. Love does not forget. Love is constant through physical lives and deaths. Your soul wants to heal and reclaim its power. These words are my gift to you in loving hope that they ignite that enchanting transformation.

To visit Jude's website www.jewellestjames.com.

To order Jewelle's first past-life book,
*All You Need Is Love*
visit www.pastlifewithjohnlennon.com

## Bibliography

Gershom, Yonassan, *Beyond the Ashes: Cases of Reincarnation from the Holocaust*, A.R.E. Press, Virginia Beach, VA., 1992.